Prasie for *Better Halves*

"This is one of those complicated and serious issues
that so many couples experience, and that only
someone who has gone through should write about
in depth. No one is more equipped to provide insight
and suggest solutions than recovering journalist
Christopher Dale. While the journey has twists and
turns, Mr. Dale always gives it to you straight."
> —Leonard Buschel, founder, Writers in Treatment
> and Editor-in-Chief, *Addiction/Recovery eBulletin*

"Christopher Dale's 'marital memoir' isn't always a
pleasure to read—no book with the line 'my weekly
unemployment checks turned into white powder'
could be—but it is a brave and thoughtful look at
how sobriety and the brutal honesty it requires can
enrich a marriage as surely as addiction can ruin it."
> —Bill Lueders, editor, *The Progressive*

"Christopher Dale knows how and why his marriage broke, and the searing honesty, unsparing detail and limitless quest for truth with which he writes *Better Halves* will be an immeasurable help to those looking at a broken life, a broken love or a broken trust, and who want help understanding how it all goes back together again."
—Gabriel Nathan, Editor-in-Chief,
OC87 Recovery Diaries

"In *Better Halves*, Christopher Dale celebrates the 'mundane miracle' of rebuilding an honest, mutually supportive relationship after active addiction. He provides practical guidance for restoring balance between partners, walking couples through the uniquely challenging but infinitely rewarding journey of sobriety and long-term recovery. With unflinching honesty, Dale expertly examines the reality of what works—and what doesn't—when mending a marriage between two people who are equal and imperfect."
—Hopetocope.com

Better Halves

CHRISTOPHER DALE

Better Halves

REBUILDING A POST-ADDICTION MARRIAGE

THORNAPPLE
PRESS

Better Halves
Rebuilding a Post-Addiction Marriage

Thornapple Press
300 – 722 Cormorant Street
Victoria, BC V8W 1P8 Canada
press@thornapplepress.ca

Thornapple Press (formerly Thorntree Press) is a brand
of Talk Science to Me Communications Inc. Our business
offices are located in the traditional, ancestral and unceded
territories of the lək̓ʷəŋən and W̱SÁNEĆ peoples.

Cover and interior design by Jeff Werner
Copy-editing by Hazel Boydell
Proofreading by Catherine Plear

Library and Archives Canada Cataloguing in Publication
Names: Dale, Christopher, author.
Title: Better halves : rebuilding a post-addiction marriage /
   Christopher Dale.
Names: Dale, Christopher, author.
Identifiers:
   Canadiana (print) 2022026483X | Canadiana (ebook) 20220264880 |
   ISBN 9781778242045 (softcover) | ISBN 9781778242052 (EPUB) |
   ISBN 9781778242069 (Kindle) | ISBN 9781778242076 (PDF)
Subjects: LCSH: Dale, Christopher—Family. | LCSH: Recovering
   addicts—Family relationships. | LCSH:
Addicts—Family relationships. | LCSH: Marriage—
   Psychological aspects.
Classification: LCC HV4998 .D34 2022 | DDC 362.29086/55—dc23

CONTENTS

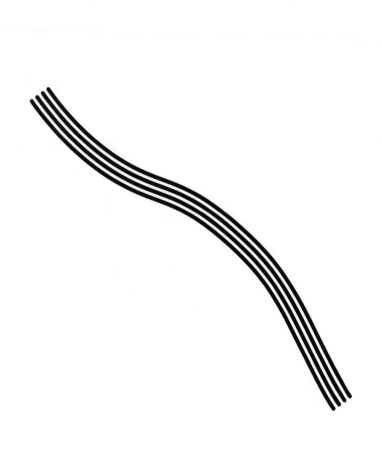

INTRODUCTION

This is not a book about drinking and drugging, nor about recovery from addiction. It will not dwell on inglorious war stories of debauchery, nor overly glorify the cessation of this self-destruction. Most accounts of debasing oneself to near-death are pointless voyeurism, and I am no hero for saving my own life.

However, as this book is intended to help recovering addicts and their significant others, some account of my background as a formerly active addict—a qualification, as members of Alcoholics Anonymous might call it—is necessary. Absent a PhD, offering advice on matters relating to addiction and recovery requires some establishing of my bona fides as both a progressively desperate addict and, today, a grateful recovering one.

Similarly, some background on my wife and our relationship is required as a point of reference and, I hope, identification. I will tackle these prerequisites here and in the ensuing Prologue to minimize backtracking and tangents in subsequent chapters.

My name is Chris, and I'm a recovering alcoholic and drug addict. My drink of choice was cheap beer; my drug of choice was expensive cocaine. I have been clean and sober since October 2011.

My story has twists and turns that, for drunks and junkies, almost always lead to the same place: a hard, low bottom. But for starters it checks at least one cliché: my childhood was a difficult one.

The daughter of two alcoholics, my mother married at 19, had me at 21 and died, seven months pregnant with what would have been my younger sister, at 24. My father, the son of an alcoholic dad who died of cirrhosis, either never really recovered from my mother's death or never possessed the nurturing skills necessary for fatherhood. It was likely a combination of these factors that influenced his parenting.

Before I check off another cliché—an addict bashing his parents—let me say that, today, my father is in my life. He is a loving grandfather to my son and a doting grand-paw to my rescue dog. He is a regular at my house, and a fixture of my household. Though our relationship didn't start well, it didn't end badly—or end, period.

My father's weak spot wasn't love, but rather guidance. This wasn't his fault, because you can't give something you don't possess. Raised in craziness, my father did well to graduate college, begin what would develop into a near-40-year career, and marry a lovely, attractive woman in my mother. But asking him to raise a child alone, from age 30, after finding his pregnant wife suddenly dead in bed one day was a bridge too far, and it left us both drowning.

My inadequate upbringing was more a matter of circumstance than malice or even incompetence. I grew up socially awkward, an unease either caused or exacerbated by the knowledge that most of my peers lived in nice houses, and had two parents and siblings, whereas my apartment-dwelling, only child, son-of-a-widower experience had none of these normalcies.

All this led to a deep-rooted inferiority complex that I would carry into adulthood. It was as if everyone else had been given an operating manual for life that was denied me; my peers seemed to possess a nurture-instilled normalcy derived from their comparably conventional home lives. Though not decidedly unpopular—I had friends and even girlfriends—there was an anxious alienation that only deepened throughout adolescence as friends and classmates built a foundation of traditional family experiences that were, and to some extent remain, foreign to me.

My response—a reasonable one, in retrospect—was to flee for somewhere unconventional. While most of my classmates went to state or private universities with traditional campuses, I opted for New York University's blend of reputation and relative anonymity. It felt safer being a square peg there.

And that, I think, would have been the beginning of the end for the more debilitating of my emotional detriments. Would have.

I found a niche and a groove at NYU. After a brief false start toward computer science, one abruptly abandoned upon earning a 12 on a calculus midterm (yes, out of 100), I realized my skills were with words rather than numbers. I switched majors to journalism, which was fortunate as NYU is highly respected in that field.

Then, in the fall of 1998, my sophomore year, I met the love of my life—Patricia. Ironically enough given my non-conformist comforts, it was at a frat-worthy party at Rutgers (New Jersey's enormous state university), where she was a student and I was visiting a high school friend.

So I was young and in love in New York City, attending a great school and with a major that matched my forte. My unhappy childhood was poised to transition into a content, promising early adulthood. I graduated with honors and entered the workforce.

And then I started losing my eyesight.

Yes, this is where my life took the sharp left turn that led, however indirectly, to alcoholism and addiction. For 18 months, a team of doctors with increasingly multisyllabic titles conducted visual field exams, CAT scans, MRIs, bloodwork and even a spinal tap in an attempt to discover why my optic nerve seemed to be rotting out of my skull.

All the while, my corrected vision incrementally declined from 20/20 to 20/30, 20/40, 20/50. One doctor thought I had multiple sclerosis, another said I'd likely go mostly blind. Several others, after ruling out their initial suspicions, posited no diagnosis-by-elimination whatsoever.

Right around 20/60, corrected and with large blind spots in both eyes, my eyesight suddenly stabilized. I didn't need a doctor to know it had stabilized, because when you're steadily losing something as vital as vision, you know pretty quickly when you've stopped losing it. Despite the lack of a satisfying medical explanation, the remainder of my eyesight had been spared, at least for the time being.

What hadn't been spared was my psyche. Perhaps someone with a solid foundation—a young adult raised right and without a penchant for panic—could have weathered such a prolonged assault on his nerves. Perhaps not.

Humans take in about 90 percent of the information around them through their eyes. So while fear of losing one's eyesight isn't an excuse to completely unravel, it's hard to argue that it isn't a viable reason. But it is equally difficult to believe that my unpreparedness for adulthood—the lack of a solid foundation acquired through adequate childrearing—did not also play a significant role.

It was a killer combo: My formative years had been insufficiently informative, and something truly traumatic had occurred in early adulthood. I didn't know how to process the anxiety and approach the work needed to overcome it. So I did what came naturally to an already-alienated person emerging from an inherently alienating experience: I tried to move on without any idea of how to do so.

I was OK for a while. I rededicated myself to work, reconnected with some long-ignored friends and generally tried to reengage with life. I got a place in Brooklyn. I got a promotion or two. I got engaged to Patty and, in April 2007, we married.

But things weren't connected, or normal. They weren't OK. I was too anxious and ill-equipped to operate as an adult in the real world. I was faking it to make it, glomming cues and hints from other adults in an attempt to grow up via osmosis. And that only took me so far before it took me down.

Or rather, up. As in not sleeping up. As in not sleeping, at all, for a week up. In January 2007, three months before my wedding day, I was in the hospital, an exhausted, emaciated skeleton of a man-child. I was hallucinating and openly contemplating suicide, and not necessarily in that order.

Nobody would have blamed Patty for bailing at that point. She didn't. Though if she'd known that this was a stroll in the park compared to what was coming, she may have.

After the wedding, I tried, again unsuccessfully, to assimilate into some semblance of normalcy—this time as a newly-married man (hey, what's more normal than that?). This is when my alcohol consumption began to increase substantially. For starters, it helped calm my nerves. For finishers, it helped me sleep.

And in between, it yanked me out of myself. Or, at least, quieted the steady, oftentimes shouting voice in my head perpetually telling me that I either didn't belong or wasn't good enough. That was two more clichés in one sentence, and here's another: Alcohol saved my life before it helped ruin it. It's better to drink on the fire escape than jump off it.

I was drinking nearly every day. On workdays, 5:30 pm couldn't come fast enough. On weekends, the same could be said for noon. Luckily, brunch is big in bourgeois Brooklyn.

I was in my late 20s and well on my way to becoming a full-blown alcoholic. Booze was starting to drive my life. Then cocaine hijacked it, took the wheel, and drove it off a cliff.

To someone who'd been so insecure for so long, introducing something as euphoric as cocaine to the brain chemistry had a predictable result. I had never felt anything close to the rush of dopamine bliss that cocaine gave. It was a figurative powder keg of pleasure, and I was near-instantly addicted.

Here again, cocaine probably saved my life before it ruined it. For one, it ripped the Band-Aid off the open wound that was my life, forcing me to either apply a sturdier tourniquet or bleed out entirely. Cocaine made the wringer of addiction far harsher than alcohol alone would have. (At least for me—this is not a drug-of-choice pissing contest. For some people alcohol can be debilitating quite quickly. To each his own poison.)

Thankfully, cocaine also made active addiction *briefer* than it would have been with alcohol alone. I'm not sure if I'd still be drinking had I not discovered cocaine, but I certainly wouldn't have over a decade of sobriety. I'd have four years, or one. Or none. Or I'd be divorced, and therefore not writing the book you're currently reading. Perhaps I'd be dead in a drunk-driving accident, or in prison for killing someone else in similar fashion. Addiction carries a broad spectrum of disparate, uneven potential consequences; the less time a person spends in active abuse, the better their chances of avoiding the worst of them.

So yes, cocaine was a catalyst that expedited my delivery to recovery. But on the other side of the coin was what members of Alcoholics Anonymous see as the three possible end games of unarrested addiction: jails, institutions and death. But again, we're not here for war stories. The story of how my life, and especially my marriage, was put back together is far more engaging and, I hope, more helpful.

Suffice to say that cocaine addiction took me on a steep, sharp spiral. I hit the bottom hard, and scuttled along the canyon floor for a while before starting my long, infinitely fulfilling uphill trudge to recovery.

A one-paragraph summary of my cocaine career: Three years. Roughly $100,000, including a cashed in 401(K) plan and several maxed out credit cards. Unemployed, then unemployable. A really good liar, then an increasingly sloppy one. Volatile in character but predictable in action. Nearly divorced several times, and *really* nearly divorced once.

My addiction did not go quietly into the night. I drove up every avenue, stumbled down every street and crept through every alleyway along my narrowing roadmap to drinking and drugging without suffering unsustainable, steadily worsening consequences. As my affliction reached its disastrous depths, it took too much alcohol and cocaine for me to get drunk and high without Patty nailing me nearly every time.

And then, mercifully, it—or rather, I—was done, courtesy of the New York City Police Department. My last drink came shortly before sideswiping a taxi in the Holland Tunnel connecting New York and New Jersey, en route to my cop spot in Manhattan. Instead of copping, I got copped: arrested for drunk driving and fleeing the scene of an accident. It was about as soft a landing as someone who'd been at it that hard could expect. A night in the drunk tank, suspended driver's license and a fed-up spouse.

Despite multiple threats of leaving me over the previous few years, somehow I knew that, this time, Patty meant it. On top of that, I had recently managed to get a new, well-paying job.

I didn't want to lose my wife nor another well-paying job to addiction, and with my license suspended I now had no escape vehicle to boot. I was scared stiff and stuck inside. And it was just enough to make a proper go of it.

There was no ray of white light, no parting of the sea, no moment of clarity. I entered recovery in a cage, with no leeway on which to rely or roadway on which to escape. Some people are 99 percent certain that they want to get sober when they finally show up at a program of recovery like Alcoholics Anonymous. I was 51 percent, tops.

Of the many things this book isn't, it's also not an infomercial for Alcoholics Anonymous/Narcotics Anonymous (same program, different name) as the sole means of recovery. I'm sure there are many appropriate, sustainable paths to longstanding recovery. The 12 Steps of Alcoholics Anonymous just happen to be mine.

Despite an agnosticism that still lingers today, I took to the stereotypically Higher Power-centric AA quite well. The men and women in those meetings with five, ten, even 20+ years free of drugs and alcohol were proof enough for me that the program worked, with or without a traditional deity in my life.

Those men included my sponsor, who took me through the 12 Steps expertly. After a few months it was clear to me that I was in the midst of a life-altering, if not lifesaving, experience that would affect every single aspect of my existence.

Existence is, mostly, a series of relationships—to our surroundings, to our unique circumstances and, especially, to other people. I would argue, then, that no part of one's existence is more significant than the one relationship we publicly profess to be permanent: the accord into which we willingly enter with a life partner or spouse.

This is the story of how two people repaired their marriage in the wake of one spouse's addiction and subsequent recovery. The messages and methods that Patty and I employed in doing so are far more important than our marital memoir, which is but a device to deliver what I hope are useful, common-sense insights. I hope that others with past experiences such as ours can join us in our present: as a happy, healthy union.

PROLOGUE

"I don't care if we have to pin him down like a mental patient. It's our fucking job."

That was me, in December 2018, sharing my enlightened views on medicine administration with my wife, Patty. Our two-year-old, Nicholas, had pneumonia, and the issue at hand was getting a screaming, persistently puking toddler to swallow foul-tasting antibiotics.

I should have put it more politely. But I didn't, and that's not the point. The point is that I didn't have to.

Because today our marriage, against historically high odds, is a solid partnership. We have tell-each-other-off credit—the type a marriage needs when a sick kid won't take his meds and your spouse is concocting complicated elixirs ("Maybe he'll drink it with Gatorade!") instead of employing a more fitting tactic: in this case, brute force. A marriage doesn't need perfect tranquility. Day-to-day life, especially once kids enter the picture, isn't about being deeply in touch with each other's feelings and desires round the clock. We don't wake up every morning trying to validate each other's hopes and dreams.

Far more crucial—and sustainable—is knowing that you can depend on a partner who you love and respect without having to tiptoe around their feelings when shit goes sideways and an immediate problem needs an immediate solution, expletives or no expletives.

This holds doubly true when it's the recovering addict doing the swearing, rather than the innocent party to addiction's indignities. It would be easy, perhaps even understandable, to conclude that I've caused Patty enough harm and heartache over the years to have relinquished the right to raise my voice to her again, ever. But marriages can't exist on eggshells.

A marriage must, first and foremost, be a partnership of equals; it simply isn't workable otherwise. Marriages have too many instances requiring frank give-and-take to withstand long-standing imbalances. And in between these mission-critical moments, marriages have too many shared struggles, responsibilities and aspirations for one partner to have the permanent upper hand.

Try it. We did, for a time. It doesn't work, because it turns the normal abnormal. It makes everyday life lopsided, a slippery slope to separation.

It is impossible to recognize how extraordinary the mundane—and even the profane—can be until you've forfeited it. There's something special in nothing special. This book is about recapturing that blissful blasé. The added gratitude for obstacles overcome, and the benefits gained by developing and honing the separate but synergistic tools of mutual recovery are an added bonus.

It's been a long, hard road to lovingly cramming antibiotics down a rampaging two-year-old's throat together with no more than a "Sorry I swore in front of Nicholas" needed to move on completely from so common a marital transgression.

Today our marriage is as normal as any can claim to be. How we got here fascinates me, and I hope it helps you.

≈

My wife and I are an odd pairing.

If you've read the introduction to this book, you've learned plenty about me: tough childhood, alienation, social anxiety, eventually alcoholism and cocaine addiction. I was raised in volatility, an unsavory trait that was only exacerbated through my 20s and early 30s as bottles of booze and bags of blow eroded whatever sanity I'd had, which wasn't much.

My wife, Patty, is the polar opposite. Stable, steady and eminently reliable, she and her younger sister grew up in a two-parent, affluent household in suburban New Jersey.

Patty's family is so normal that it's almost weird. A first-generation American, she was raised by happily married Chinese immigrants who embraced America and Americana with the passion of two people born into far fewer prospects and freedoms.

For my wife, the result was an upper-middle-class childhood punctuated by Disney, Elvis and shamelessly overdone Christmases. And above all, family. Her family has more traditional American values than most native-born Americans. They are Donna Reed meets dim sum.

Why, as a sophomore at Rutgers University in New Jersey, she fell in love with an emotionally erratic, arrogant twig is anyone's guess. All I had to offer was a fairly sharp wit and, I suppose, a modicum of book smarts to offset a complete lack of street smarts. And since I was a student at New York University, I also had a place in the city. What a catch.

Our courtship, like many courtships, wasn't linear. We dated throughout college, broke up for a while, called each other scared and crying on 9/11 (the North Tower was a subway transfer point for me, and I was under the building when the first plane hit). We tried dating without exclusivity, and found that mutual jealousy made that impossible.

She was there for me during my harrowing eyesight health scare (again, see the Introduction), and the bouts of depression and anxiety that followed in the wake of such a mortifying experience.

I was there for her because she was there for me, a loyalty forged not out of obligation but appreciation. I didn't stick by Patty merely because she'd stuck with me through difficult times; I stayed with Patty because I realized how incredible a person she was for doing so in such a loving, mature-beyond-her-years fashion.

Along the way two different, relatively rigid people bent in toward each other. Eventually our arcs were close enough that a keystone, in the form of an engagement ring, completed an arch. That was June 2006. It would be among the last good decisions I'd make before finally walking into a meeting of Alcoholics Anonymous on October 12, 2011, having recently been released from a Manhattan jail cell for a no-doubter DUI involving an inglorious hit-and-run and an even more inglorious police car pants-pissing.

Leading up to our engagement and eventual marriage, the story of Patty and Chris is not particularly intriguing. Save for the freakish health scare on my part, we were just two average people who saw enough of life together that we decided to spend the rest of it with each other rather than separately. That's not extraordinary romance; it's just ordinary love.

That vow was strained shortly thereafter. Not because of our union, but despite it, the deck-stacking combination of nature and nurture caught up with me. My difficult upbringing and frightening health issues created a short fuse, one doused in alcohol and soon sparked irrevocably by cocaine. My life exploded, and our young marriage went along with it.

Yet through three years of bottle-hiding, eight-ball-snorting hell, we endured. It wouldn't have lasted much longer had I not gotten clean. Patty is too capable and independent a person to have let it. Love held the line, but just barely.

What happened next—the reason for this book—is a mundane miracle. It's the story of how two people rebuilt an equal marriage from a starting point of near-total imbalance. This is something special. But I can't stress enough that *we are not special.*

We are not star-crossed lovers. This is not destiny or fate. We are not exceptionally compatible. In fact, compared to most couples we know, we have less in common than the average life partners. We both like to travel, have a foodie streak and see eye-to-eye on most political matters. We both cherish our (thankfully now healthy) son. We binge-watch TV, procrastinate over yard work and tolerate each other's families.

In between we bicker, with the occasional knock-down drag-out war. We can both be stubborn and, with our not-so-epic romance in its third decade, know how to push each other's buttons for maximum annoyance. I bite my nails and leave clippings on the floor like a caveman. She does this scrapy thing when eating with a spoon that makes me want to dump her yogurt on top of her precious little head.

We are nobody's idea of the perfect married couple. But we *are* a married couple. This story is about how, after one partner's steep descent into addiction and disruptive subsequent recovery, we are not only married but happily so.

In the process, Patty and I have not become perfectly compatible or fallen perfectly in love. Rather, we've arrived at a place where none of those hackneyed, unattainable ideals are necessary. We have rebuilt, stronger than ever, the foundation lost to addiction, cracked facade and all, without attempting sainthood to make up for the hell of years past. We wish the same messy, wonderfully real journey for couples following in our flawed footsteps.

Today, from a marital standpoint, the best thing that can be said about my addiction is that it seems like it happened several long decades ago rather than one short one. It is as near a non-entity, I believe, as is humanly possible for two people with nightmarish memories.

We've drained oceans of booze and dynamited mountains of cocaine. What once was everything has become nothing, the isolating barriers of the past not only reduced to rubble but pulverized and scattered in the wind.

This book is about how we arrived at this barrier-free coexistence. It's about being as unconstrained, unconcerned and unaffected as possible. It's about addiction fading so far into the past that it has all but disappeared from the present.

Some things are better off as nothings. Here goes nothing.

Part I:
Active Addiction

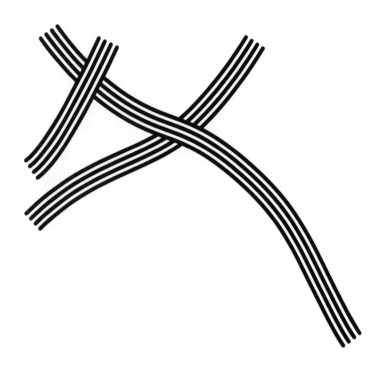

CHAPTER 1:
THE BEGINNING OF THE END

"I'm going to be a little later than usual tonight," I said. "Lots going on here at work." The first statement was certainly true, the second most certainly was not.

"OK," my wife, Patty, replied. "You alright? You sound stuffed up."

"I'm fine. A little run down. Maybe I'm catching a cold or something."

I hung up, relieved that I could now go back to pretending to work, while paying far more attention to the neat rows of cocaine lined up on a book under my desk. It was about 4:30 in the afternoon. People would start leaving the office soon, meaning I could powder my nose less clandestinely while doing...what exactly?

It was the first time I'd done it this early. Shortly after lunch, my mind began wandering along a path typically not traversed until a few drinks into happy hour. Alcohol and cocaine are as compatible, albeit in a decidedly scummier fashion, as coffee and cigarettes. My desire for blow was usually piqued only after a few beers, and almost always in a social setting.

But today was different. By about 2 pm, what I'd later discover was a mental obsession with my drug of choice sneakily manifested itself as innocent distraction. I wasn't particularly busy at work, the little voice said, and could afford to goof off this afternoon. Take it easy. Shoot some emails back and forth with friends. Play some stupid games online.

Hey, you know what's *really* fun? You have your own office. You can totally get away with it.

It was the first time that even a sliver of a thought occurred to me that this was beyond the boundaries of recreational drug use. A small part of me didn't want to do it. But a more pressing force had me fidgeting in my chair, tapping my fingers on my desk in an absent-minded, faux-piano-playing rhythm, staring not so much at my computer screen but through it.

I was calculating the logistics of the act. A phone call, a quick trip downstairs to hit the ATM and get it, concealing it under my desk. A rolled-up Post-It note would do for a delivery device. My blood began to itch. Game on.

My fingers stopped playing air piano and picked up the phone. I didn't need to search my contacts for the number—I had it memorized. In hindsight, that seems like another jarringly lucid warning sign.

After a few more rings than usual, a groggy voice answered.

"Christopher?" My drug dealer was surprisingly formal. Most people just called me Chris.

"You around, man?" I asked, as casually as possible considering that, for him, it was more like early morning on a Sunday than early afternoon on a Wednesday. His isn't exactly a 9 to 5 business model.

"Nah man. Give me like at least another hour or so. Where you at?"

Manhattan is a druggie's dream. The dealers come right to you, usually doing the handoff in a bar bathroom or someplace similar. This would be a little more public, but we'd manage. Some sort of "what's up, bro" hand-clasp chest-bump combo should do the trick.

It was also the first time I'd ever scored from my workplace, a public relations firm in East Midtown. I gave him the cross streets, hung up, and tried to work until, as far as my colleagues could discern, I'd be summoned downstairs to retrieve an urgent package from a bike messenger I was waiting on so that I could synergistically get my ducks in a row. That would, of course, require some interfacing. Back in a jiff.

Suffice to say I got what I needed to get. I spent the next hour—a timeframe that included the phony phone call to my wife—debasing myself slowly, careful not to toot too much too soon. This was a place of business, for God's sake. I literally had to keep my nose clean.

Once the last of my colleagues left, I spent the rest of the evening snorting copious amounts of cocaine off my spacious leather portfolio (#classy). My drug use had officially gone from a barroom maybe to a workplace must.

≈

It wasn't the first time I'd lied to Patty about using cocaine. After all, hard drugs (let's all agree that anything other than marijuana is a hard drug) aren't exactly the types of things people are completely forthcoming about each and every time.

Still, until now my fibs were typically late-night lies after the fact. We'd be at a party, and I'd say I'd had two small lines rather than six not-so-small ones. Certainly nothing to be proud of, but nothing so far out of the ordinary as to raise a red flag about the white stuff. I had friends who indulged as well, giving the exercise the pseudo-normalcy of a group project.

But this time was different. This time there was no bar, no house party, no friends, not even any alcohol to light the fire. This time I was completely avoiding my wife to hide and get high. Really high. Like $100 worth of coke in three hours high.

There was no real reason and no real exit strategy. After I was done snorting away in an empty office for several hours, I was going to do...what? Dust off my desk, turn off my light and take the subway home to my wife in Brooklyn? I had just performed an illegal, professionally threatening act with no forethought as to what came next. I had somehow allowed myself to completely ignore the obvious endgame: that once the drugs were gone, reality awaited.

Pinpointing addiction's exact start date is difficult, and for all intents and purposes irrelevant. I can't report with GPS-level accuracy at precisely what point I crossed over from recreational cocaine enthusiast to reprehensible cocaine junkie. I can't give an entirely accurate account of where "I'd like it" ended and "I need it" began.

What I can say for sure is that right there, that night, was the beginning of the end of true marital balance. Any union of equals, any partnership where responsibilities are shared, intentions made known and goals jointly worked toward, must be rooted in honesty. This was the day that any false pretenses between us went from white lies to dark deceptions.

From that day forward, our paths would incrementally diverge until the two starting points, our individual selves, were barely visible on each other's horizons. It was the start of a mock marriage of sorts, one where each party was living a separate existence, even if that fact was unknown to one of them.

In Patty's mind that night, she still had a loving, hardworking husband—one with faults, yes, but someone largely open and honest with her and, at the very least, someone who wouldn't do anything to intentionally harm her.

But in my own sickening psyche, Patty was becoming less of a wife and more of an obstacle, someone who stood in the way of something that was becoming more important to me than anything else: my love affair with cocaine.

At the time, of course, all of this was imperceptible to me, obliterated by the deluge of dopamine loosed by line after line, a giddy excitability that gives way to a dumbfounded numbness as the dosage increases. Cocaine gave me fake happiness followed by actual obliviousness.

Cocaine provided an instant break from the anxiety and depression I had battled since early adulthood, when the combination of a difficult childhood and a freak health scare had left my psyche fragile. (My optic nerve had partially deteriorated—see the Introduction for the full story.) I was sick and tired of being nervous and scared. Cocaine was the ultimate pain reliever.

I don't remember exactly how that night I first did cocaine in the office ended. Though there's no such thing as a "whiteout," there were just so many nights from there that ended in similar anticlimactic fashion that the memories simply blend. Most likely I stumbled in the door around 9 pm, said I wasn't feeling too well (hey, I *had* been noticeably stuffed up on the phone earlier, right?), and pretended to sleep while my poisoned bloodstream and racing heart made doing so a fool's errand.

≈

From that evening onward, our marriage was no longer a union of equals. So disruptive a force is addiction that no relationship can sustain anything resembling balance for any significant stretch of time. Even if it doesn't ultimately dissolve, any marriage where one (or both) partners is compulsively abusing substances is a failed one.

I know of no exceptions to that rule. In over a decade of recovery I've yet to witness, or even hear about, any content couple in which one spouse is waging an indefinite battle with addiction. If you think you're that couple, think again.

Certainly, Patty and I are no exception. That phone call on a random work night signified that addiction had, ever so slightly, begun to step on the previously reasonably even scales of our relationship. For balance to have so much as the possibility of being restored, my physical addiction would need to be broken and replaced by complete and total abstinence from drugs and alcohol.

All burgeoning addicts must run a dangerous gauntlet, either dying in the middle or emerging having overcome grievous adversity. Unfortunately, married addicts drag their spouses through an emotional equivalent of their physical, spiritual trial. Recovery from addiction would depend on my emerging bloodied but unbeaten. Our marriage's survival would depend on my wife's willingness to accept unfairly inflicted mental scars, to mend whatever was reparable and, from there, forgive what she couldn't forget.

So here Patty and I were, at this grand gauntlet's entrance, our partnership tipped off-kilter with no recalibration in sight. To achieve the rebalancing act that was now vital to our marriage's survival, my recovery from addiction was not the solution but rather the *prerequisite* to the solution—one I would fail to meet for another three brutal years.

Let's pause for a moment to address a question I've gotten from both fellow addicts and regular folks: Why three years? The answer is that three years is a completely arbitrary, random timeframe. That's simply when I was finally ready to permanently put the bags away and the bottles down.

Non-addicts (or "normies," as they are sometimes referred to as in AA meetings) might see this as a lengthy period of time. More often than not, fellow addicts and especially alcoholics see my run in active addiction as relatively brief. For addicts whose drug of choice is alcohol, their runs are often far longer than mine. But for those, like me, whose primary problem was with hard drugs, the spiral of addiction is often steeper.

What cocaine did, more than anything, was rip the already-porous bandage off my addiction. It hastened what had begun, via alcohol, as a slow yet steady bleed. I have no doubt that, eventually, my alcoholism would have brought me to the same insane, insufferable condition as cocaine. But what cocaine did is made the gauntlet of addiction both fiercer and, thankfully, shorter. Over a more condensed period of time, I was either going to die or be desperate enough to get and remain clean and sober.

The point of this digression is that addiction's course is highly customized, an odd facet for a "takes one to know one" affliction whose treatment thrives on identification with fellow sufferers. Each alcoholic and addict reaches his or her bottom over a personal timeframe. And certainly, our bottoms themselves look different. For some, all it takes to birth sobriety is a wakeup call blackout while she still has a husband, a house and a job. For most, myself included, the bottom is far deeper. And unfortunately, for many the bottom is death.

Returning to the context of marriages where one partner is an addict, an apt metaphor for the ailment's progression is a fork in the road that, from its inception, forces spouses to take different paths. At first, the roads seem similar enough and, since each spouse is still near the point at which the road split, reasonably close to each other. They may even seem parallel. Hey look Patty, there's Chris. I'm sure the roads reconnect shortly.

But as time passes and the incurable malady of addiction progresses, the roads not only continue to diverge but begin to independently deteriorate. What was originally smooth pavement starts to be pocked with potholes and, soon enough, it gives way to gravel and, eventually, dirt. The roads narrow and bend further from each other, running east and west respectively where before they led true north.

The roads compress further, and begin to be partially obstructed by overgrowth. An incline starts, barely noticeable at first but quickly becoming what appears to be a 45-degree ascent with no level ground in sight.

Over an extended timeline, what eventually happens in this scenario is predictable: at least one of the two spouses—let's say the non-addicted wife—simply stops walking. She looks around, wonders how the hell she ended up so lost and alone, does an about-face and begins her descent. The road gets wider, less obstructed, more paved. She comes to the point of the original fork and, fed up with the whole endeavor, simply keeps walking. Whether or not her husband wandered down that other path no longer matters. Her journey is over.

In this metaphor, the only occurrence that can start to turn the roads back toward each other—and keep them from becoming increasingly impassable—is the complete and longstanding cessation of drugs and alcohol by the addicted partner. This does not guarantee that the two roads will ever connect again—it merely makes that reconvergence a possibility.

These first few chapters are about the lonely, treacherous trudge that is a marriage impacted by active addiction.

$$\approx$$

In the earliest stages of addiction, the balance of power tilts toward the addict. As cocaine tightened its grip on me, I tightened my grip on Patty. As I fabricated scenarios that provided the time to isolate and use cocaine, she was, unknowingly, increasingly living in a fantasy world where her husband worked late hours (how diligent and dedicated!) and was suddenly hanging out with long-estranged acquaintances again (how outgoing and gregarious!).

The excuses an addict makes to his spouse are an attempt at plausible Mad Libs. "Do you remember (insert phantom friend here)? Haven't seen him in a while and wanted to catch up. We're (insert believable activity here) on (insert non-suspicious timeframe here). That OK?"

This all happens under the umbrella of one truth: addicts and alcoholics are, typically, liars. This isn't by design, but rather necessity.

At some nebulous point—the office escapade that opened this chapter, for example—a problem drinker or substance abuser reaches the point where their drinking or drugging becomes abnormal. Upon noticing this, the addict realizes that they cannot continue to feed their addiction while living honestly within the expectations of the world: society, employers, family and friends.

The only conceivable (albeit inevitably short-sighted) solution is to become a liar, usually a pretty damn good one. Addiction is a condition whose symptoms—obsessive, compulsive drinking and drugging—are fundamentally at odds with living truthfully. We have to lie to keep drinking and using the way we want to, the way we *have to*, drink and use.

This is not to excuse the addict's behavior. All people are responsible, and ultimately must be held accountable, for their actions whether they are sober as a judge or drunk and high in front of one. Rather, this is simply to show the overarching truth that active addicts and alcoholics are, by the nature of their affliction, usually accomplished liars.

It is also to show that this addiction-driven untruthfulness stems from a place of necessity rather than malice. This is an important, even vital realization for spouses of both active and recovering addicts, and we will return to this concept in subsequent scenarios.

The reason it is so necessary for spouses to understand this is because they bear the brunt of these lies. Patty was more personally invested in me, and more *in my way*, than any other person, place or thing standing between me and my predetermined need to excessively drink or drug.

Years later, Patty would ask me why I lied to her so early, so often, so effectively. The answer is the same reason a mountaineer gives to a recently conquered peak: "Because you were there."

I lied because she was a detriment to doing what I needed to do, a statement that is simultaneously cruel and comforting. It really had nothing to do with Patty. I would have lied to anyone about anything to do what my addiction was compelling me to do.

But that, of course, doesn't make this most personal of betrayals sting any less. Our spouses are, by nature, the ones who know us most. We are invested in and familiar with our spouses on a more intimate level than any other relationship. Ideally, a spouse is the love of your life and a best friend rolled into one. We know each other's turn-ons and turn-offs, fortes and weaknesses, idiosyncrasies and blind spots. We come to know intuitively what the other is thinking merely from the slightest sigh, facial feign or glance—mundane gestures imperceptible to anyone else on this planet except each other.

Back in my insert-excuse-here early addiction, all this would be used against Patty. Or rather, for me. Because unintentionally, what the spouses of active addicts become is a litmus test for fooling the rest of the world. It's terrible but true: Patty was the perfect patsy.

For married couples, another harsh reality emerges: the addicted spouse learns to lie more quickly and effectively by the mere circumstance of marriage. As the person who both knew me better than anyone else, and who lived with me and was therefore most often an obstacle to finding the time, place and means to use, Patty was an unwitting accomplice in honing my burgeoning bullshitting skills. If I could fool her, I figured, I could fool anyone.

This is, let's all agree, very fucked up. I'm cringing as I write this. I can only imagine what you're thinking reading it. But the plain and simple truth is that I used Patty as a tool to sharpen my ability to lie effortlessly, effusively and effectively.

I became an excellent liar and, though that is by no means Patty's fault, I certainly can assign her with partial credit. Like any skill, lying takes practice, and the very presence of a spouse makes practice more necessary and available to a married addict as opposed to a bachelor.

On a day-to-day basis, what that looked like was a shameful master class in deceit. In very early addiction most addicts, myself included, still have a nearly full tool-box of faculties and resources. In addition to the condo Patty and I owned, I had a job, a car (with a valid driver's license!), friends, money in the bank, credit cards with high limits and low balances. Nobody suspected me of anything more serious than, perhaps, being an excitable jerk who sometimes overdid it at the bar.

Just as importantly, addiction hadn't completely warped my concept of reality yet. It hadn't robbed me of my intelligence, reason or ability to place myself in someone else's shoes—all crucial elements to concocting believable falsehoods.

What the combination of assets, acumen and addiction amounts to is *leverage*. I had every reason to lie and every possible way to get away with it.

Addiction is a blur that is too manic and frantic for flawless self-analysis, even with the benefit of long-standing sobriety and years of therapy. However,

I would contend that the assets I had available at the very beginning of addiction's grasp hastened my disease's progression.

Think about it: when you have the ability to get away with something as all-consuming as the compulsive need to do mountains of cocaine, you tend to…well, do mountains of cocaine. If necessity is the mother of invention, opportunity is the father of success. Since I had easy opportunities to successfully feed my addiction, feed it I did. And when you feed an obsession, what happens is predictable: it grows.

Here, Patty was more an asset than a constraining liability. Part of this is circumstantial: I had an office to hide in, phantom friends to conspire with and separate checking and credit card accounts to fund my debauchery.

But another aspect here is inherent to the institution of marriage. We've already discussed how a spouse becomes an unwitting trainer for an addict's lying prowess. What a spouse also does is *keep the addict honest enough to continue being dishonest.*

The need to keep up appearances with Patty made me keep up appearances elsewhere. The simple fact of being married made me adapt my addiction to my domestic surroundings, an exercise in believability that I would deepen and draw upon until the well of goodwill was completely parched.

It can be argued that this slowed the disease's progression by putting some baseline constraints on what I could and could not get away with. Though this may be true, it also taught me how to normalize my addiction in a way that best hid it from everyone, Patty included. Marriage, which was supposed to make me a better man, merely made me a better addict.

Oh, the roles I played! We'll dive deeper into this in the next chapter, but let's briefly touch upon a few recurring characters.

First, in the early days of my addiction I became a truly dedicated yet inundated executive. As far as Patty was concerned, business was really booming with new clients and newly demanding existing ones. I frequently fake-complained that it was really getting ridiculous. If the deluge of work continued for much longer I'd have to seriously consider looking for another job.

In reality, my desk was certainly the center of a hell of a lot of activity. It held the large, flat-screen monitor behind which I hid, pretending to work. It also hid, in its top drawer or at my feet, the afternoon's voluminous supply of blow.

Outside the office, my social life was expanding exponentially. As far as Patty knew, I was at a sports bar watching the game with some buddies. In reality, I was at a dive bar chugging cheap beer and disappearing to a bathroom that locked every five minutes to, um, take a piss. Boy did that beer seem to go right through me.

And of course, there were the times when I couldn't get away. The times when I had to figure out how to get the cocaine up my nose right under my wife's nose. The times I would feign insomnia to escape to the couch. The unnecessary loads of laundry that suddenly needed urgent attention. The trips to the bathrooms with the shits (or, more accurately, the bullshits). These instances, perhaps, are the most offensive of all to Patty because, in hindsight, she feels not only betrayed and belittled but naive and foolish.

Here, we arrive at another important point that any couple trying to regain balance must understand: None of this is the non-addict spouse's fault, at all, period. If you're reading this as a newly recovering addict or the spouse of one, take the word "enabler" and remove it from your vocabulary. It is a useless word that is too often employed to deflect blame and, even where somewhat applicable, rarely serves to help a marriage repair once physical sobriety has been accomplished by the addicted partner.

Regardless, to this day Patty has a hard time dealing with a sentiment that, in her mind, is something along the lines of "How could I have missed all this? How could I have been so blind, so stupid?"

This is a false flag emotion. It is Patty essentially blaming herself for giving the person she most loved in the world the benefit of the doubt for as long as she could. It's her rationalizing that she might have saved us both a lot of pain had she been more suspicious earlier than she ultimately was. It is her asking the impossible of herself. It is, essentially, Patty blaming herself for loving her own husband. Even now, after all the grief and humiliation and debt I caused her, this self-loathing mental anguish I caused Patty is among the hardest pills for me to swallow.

But swallow it I—*we*—must. Restoring balance in the wake of addiction and recovery doesn't always mean having a complete solution to every harm inflicted, every emotion felt, every wrong unrighted. It has far more to do with understanding the dynamics of manipulation, control and imbalance that played out in various stages, working toward amending those inequities, and making conscious decisions as a couple never to revisit them.

As we've explored, in the earliest stages of active addiction the balance of power bends toward the addict.

This is because the addict is the unassuming aggressor, a manipulator whose spouse, at first, has little reason to suspect of being manipulative.

As a result, the addict has both the motivation and opportunity to create an alternate reality for his spouse—one that buys him time to isolate and drink and drug away without anybody looking over his shoulder.

Let's explore the alternate universes created by alcoholics and addicts to distract, disorient and dissuade their spouses from learning the awful truth. Welcome to Fantasyland, population one.

CHAPTER 2:
FANTASYLAND

"Just to be clear, we're hiring somebody else."

That was Mark, the Chief Financial Officer at my office, with whom I had a pretty good relationship. He was among the last of my colleagues who could stand the sight of me, probably because we collaborated so infrequently. The fact that I was volatile and he was 200+ pounds and well over six feet tall, I'm sure, also factored into Mark drawing this particular assignment on this particular day.

That day was March 10, 2010, and that assignment was firing me.

In hindsight, I appreciate the way Mark put it. With the country mired in the Great Recession, it would have been easy for the unacceptably unreliable professional I'd become to convince himself that this dismissal reflected an unprecedented economic downturn. But with eight gut-wrenchingly direct words, Mark made it evident that this was a matter of replacement rather than redundancy. Come Monday, a new executive would occupy my office, service my accounts, earn my paycheck.

Next came among the most embarrassing moments of my life: Mark escorted me back to my office to grab some personal items including a mess of empty bottles concealed in my desk drawers, filing cabinet and God knows where else. One last dazed, pathetic attempt to save face at work, this time in looming, permanent absentia. My messenger bag clicked and clanked as I plodded, defeated, toward the exit.

Once outside, my first phone call was to Patty.

"I got laid off today."

In the coming months, I would go from unemployed to unemployable. As my weekly unemployment checks quickly turned into white powder, my workforce viability just as quickly turned to dust. I wouldn't hold another job for over a year.

But at that moment, the alternate universe I had created for Patty's sole occupancy still provided enough space for me to believably incur a sizable consequence of addiction—the loss of a job—without her recognizing addiction as the cause. Though by this time aware I had difficulty staying away from cocaine, Patty was unaware how far my addiction had progressed. Armed with incomplete information, and wanting to be supportive of her husband getting bad news in a bad economy, she was giving me the benefit of the doubt; specifically, doubt that I myself had planted in her head.

When it comes to keeping spouses off their increasingly telltale trails, married addicts become druggie deities capable of creating entire worlds where half-truths serve as foundations for flat-out falsehoods. Addiction is a long-term illness with short-term goals. Fueled by the desperate need to keep drinking and drugging in secret, my daily deceptions built a running counternarrative that led Patty down a rabbit hole until fact and fiction were intentionally indistinguishable.

In Chapter 3 we'll explore what happens when that fantasyland finally crumbles—when the addict's spouse puts enough of the pieces together to realize the severity of the problem. For now, let's look at how these alternate universes are gradually and opportunistically designed, and how their gravitational pull can be strong enough to trap even a spouse as otherwise savvy as mine.

≈

In short order, we're going to get into some pretty damning details here. Some of the hijinks I pulled leading up to getting "laid off" (with extreme prejudice) blew past mere red flags into flashing neon signs that might as well have read "WARNING: Your husband is a hopeless addict!"

The ensuing set of questions is as understandable as it is misguided. It goes something like this: How did it take my wife so long to realize the severity of my addiction? How can you live with someone—even share a bed with him—and not put the clues together? How did so much cocaine get up my nose right under Patty's nose?

Let's start with a statement you'll have to take at face value: my wife is really smart. Like straight-A student, full scholarship to a reputable college, six-figure marketing executive smart. She is also personable. Though certainly an introvert, throughout her life Patty has had healthy relationships with friends, colleagues and, before me, boyfriends.

She is also very straightforward. She's not a game player. She has a lack of coyness and mystique some might find boring but I find refreshing.

That's Patty in two paragraphs: intelligent, amiable, high-functioning, direct, clear-eyed.

At several points in this book, I'll portray Patty as an intriguing case study for this narrative. In this instance, I believe we'd be hard-pressed to find a spouse more capable of shining a light on her addict husband's shadow existence.

Somewhat vainly, I also shudder to imagine the capers I could have put over on a spouse less competent than Patty. Perhaps I would have died before being fully exposed. Unfortunately, I wouldn't have been the first to suffer such a fate—one that, however unfairly, yields a bewildering bereavement in which surviving spouses are often left undeservedly kicking themselves for not seeing the warning signs sooner.

The point is that if someone as able as Patty could be kept in the dark for as long as she was, any spouse is susceptible to being fooled for an extended period. Blaming the spouse of an addict for not discovering the full extent of her partner's alcoholism or addiction is akin to blaming an attractive woman in a skirt for getting sexually assaulted. Spouse-shaming replaces "look what she was wearing" with "look what he was doing," diverting fault from offender to victim.

Was there enough smoke to warrant pulling the fire alarm? You bet there was. Suspiciously long cigarette breaks (long enough to, say, meet my dealer), abnormally high credit card statements (read: cash advances for cocaine) and frequent, sudden work-skipping sicknesses were enough to raise anyone's eyebrows, Patty's included.

But with married addicts, where there's smoke there's smoke screen. Addicts are awfully good at throwing wet blankets on seemingly bright, burning evidence of their substance abuse.

In their ongoing gambit to conceal the depths of their condition's progression from their spouse, the addict has three inherent advantages. Combined, they explain why someone as astute as Patty was unable to see the full extent of the damage unfolding before her eyes.

Advantage #1: Shared personal history

Typically, marriages that experience one partner's alcoholism or drug addiction do not bear that cross at the union's inception. Though many alcoholics may have been hard drinkers and many eventual drug addicts enthusiastic dabblers leading up to their full-blown substance dependence, rare is the case when a normie walks down the aisle with an emergency-level drunk or drug user.

Many alcoholics and addicts go into marriage showing little more than a penchant for occasionally overdoing it at the bar. Some have even cleaner backgrounds than that. Suffice to say that most alcoholics and addicts aren't in all-out chemical dependence upon taking their vows. "I got married near my bottom" isn't a phrase regularly heard in the rooms of Alcoholics Anonymous or other group recovery settings.

This was precisely the case with Patty and me. When we married in April 2007, each just turned 28, my drinking and drug use were within the realm of normalcy for a guy who enjoyed New York City nightlife and who had friends who did as well. I wasn't an outlier by any stretch. As explained in the Introduction, my major malfunction prior to marriage was a depression-anxiety episode that left me borderline suicidal and hospitalized for exhaustion. But at the time I got married, I took anti-depressants, and a guy with a nervous composition throwing a few back once in a while seemed more fitting than foreboding.

Add to this the fact that Patty and I had dated for nearly a decade before marrying, and the history we shared painted a Chris in Patty's mind that, despite mental health issues, didn't include the likelihood of alcoholism or drug addiction. Most of us don't get married on a whim. By the time we tied the knot, I was a known commodity to Patty.

Understandably, we place our spouses on pedestals. After all, your spouse is the one person you decide is worthy of taking a vow before family and friends to love, honor and cherish forever. Our wedding days create idyllic still frames in our minds, reminding us through thick and thin of the value of the person we married and the vows we took. And at least partly due to our egos, as the marriage moves forward, the leeway extended to our spouse reflects our own reluctance to entertain the notion that our choice of life partner wasn't as perfect as we'd like to think.

As it became evident to Patty that all was not right with me, that *something* was wrong, our history together came back to haunt her. My progressing addiction prompted more elaborate schemes to keep using in isolation and anonymity, and my behavior was becoming more erratic. However, Patty was able to point to the still-remaining bright spots—my continued employment chief among them—and chock the rest up to a proclivity for depression and anxiety she was well aware of before we wed.

Love interests don't become spouses by creating unpleasant memories. Our spouses occupy a singularly favorable space in our mind's eye—a specialness that can unfortunately become a blind spot when one partner descends into alcoholism or drug addiction. Even as my actions grew increasingly more alarming, this history allowed Patty, however counterproductively, to point to a happier time waiting to be recaptured once I got my head on straight again. This marital muscle memory creates a sort of wistful wishful thinking, exacerbating our inability to consider the worst about a spouse's circumstances.

Advantage #2: Love (and not that other thing)

This section will introduce what for many might seem like a controversial issue, so let's start with the least controversial statement possible: Married couples love each other.

We put up with a lot of headaches from the people we love. We go out of our way to help them. We support them financially, emotionally, professionally, spiritually. We openly forgive them. We allow them to inconvenience, distress and upset us. "You're lucky I love you" is a common phrase that sometimes comes with an implied extension: "...or else I wouldn't be putting up with this."

We love many people in our lives but, in monogamous marriages, our spouse is the one person we've publicly agreed to love, forbidding all other romantic interests, until death breaks that most special of bonds.

Considering this, in the context of alcoholism and drug addiction, the inability of society to discuss marital love without in the same breath mentioning "codependence" is, quite frankly, just plain silly. The liberalness with which that term gets applied to two people who've publicly pledged themselves to each other grossly over-simplifies the nuptial relationship.

We'll dive deeper into this in subsequent chapters, including a discussion of how and why a spouse might stick by their addicted partner even through a bottom as low as mine, as Patty did. For now, it's enough to question (and in my opinion identify) such a sweeping spousal label as unbecoming of the depth and intricacies of the love that can exist between two married people.

There's a reason they call us life partners. That Patty first gave me the benefit of the doubt—and once that doubt was impossible to give any longer, every opportunity to turn my life around—doesn't make her codependent. In assessing spousal reactions to alcoholic or drug-addicted partners, too many professionals claim to understand where healthy love ceases and unhealthy codependency commences.

For the purposes of this limited discussion, it's enough to understand that people who love each other tend to believe, support and root for each other. Let's also recognize that alcoholics and addicts have ways of utilizing these good tidings to muddy the marital waters in increasingly egregious attempts to keep their progressing addiction incognito.

The hard truth is that addicts use their spouses' love against them, not through out and out rancor but rather insidious deception. For addicts, love is just another currency—an item of value that can be drawn upon to continue drinking and drugging the way we need to.

Advantage #3: Motivation

Never underestimate the ability of addicts to find ways of accomplishing their first priority: drinking and drugging. As our sickness progresses, getting our substances of choice into our bodies becomes a regular, oftentimes daily prerequisite. As we cross the line into addiction, we go from fitting using into our lives to fitting our lives into using.

At least subconsciously, most of us know we're addicts well before we try to get help. In my case, as I went from knowing I couldn't say no to cocaine to knowing I needed to *actively seek* it every few days, it became evident that, were I to continue living like this for the foreseeable future, I'd need more than a few cover stories here and there. I needed a rolling masquerade to hide behind lest my perpetually powdered nose be revealed.

As addiction started to take hold, then, I created running false narratives with the long view in mind. I made blanket excuses that I could return to repeatedly as reasons for otherwise inexplicable absences, withdrawn funds and peculiar behavior.

There's a timing element to this: such future-centric falsehoods are generally concocted in the period where an addict knows they are an addict but hasn't yet been brought to their knees by addiction. They still have a job, some money in the bank, and at least most of their wits about him—all of which will be utilized to create a believable buffer zone between them and the person most likely to bust up their substance abuse plans: their spouse.

A determined addict can accomplish an awful lot in altering the perspective of an unsuspecting spouse. Let's look at Patty's particular trip down the rabbit hole, dug by yours truly one shovelful of bullshit at a time.

≈

In the opening chapter we previewed some of the false narratives that fueled my audience-of-one fantasy. A prolonged busy stretch at work and reconnecting with old friends were two sturdy umbrellas under which smaller lies took shelter. They were foundational cover stories offering the benefit of being reasonably believable, indefinite in duration and difficult to verify without a third party going to great lengths (for example, a wife isn't going to call her husband's boss to see if her hubby is, indeed, inundated with work).

Addicts are idiot savants: typically, we're too stupid to seek help for what we know is a serious problem, but ingenious at carving out enough isolation for our illness to progress to the point of emergency. We excel at giving alcoholism and addiction enough elbow room to bring us to our knees.

Insanely, we're also good at convincing ourselves that the Fantasyland we create is the best situation for all parties—even our deceived spouses. For me, the "busy at work" motif provides a solid example. The convoluted rationale gives a look under the hood of the twisted addict brain. Welcome to Crazytown.

As my addiction progressed, the weekends became difficult to get through because, of course, I couldn't do cocaine around Patty. At some point doing just a little bit—some might call it "maintaining"—to feed my addiction while remaining relatively sober became insufficient to satisfy my ever-progressing condition. The amount of cocaine I needed to meet my addiction's demands required me to be alone, because it left me too high to function interpersonally. I basically became a mouth-breathing, chain-smoking zombie for an hour or two.

Not surprisingly, the debilitating physical state my addiction now demanded of me hindered my habits at the office during the workweek. It became harder and harder to effectively dabble for a few hours starting in the mid-afternoon until the last of my colleagues left for the night, at which point I could paint the town white, so to speak. As my addiction upped the ante on how messed up I needed to be to meet its cruel quota, maintaining with a toot here and there while the clock ticked toward 6 required deeper dips and bigger bumps. With thicker and thicker lines, I was walking on thin ice in my ongoing journey to hide my drug use from coworkers.

At this point, I needed a sizable amount of cocaine in my system about twice a week. Finding it harder and harder to use at work during the week and at home during the weekends, I did what any desperate addict would do: I flipped the script to suit the only actor that mattered. Me.

Before proceeding, it warrants noting that none of this came out of nowhere. I had been planting the seeds of this plan in Patty's head for some time, complaining about an increasingly swamped work life upon arriving home at increasingly late hours. Poor Fantasyland Chris: he was tired of missing dinner and missing his wife. Addicts are terrific at devising "poor me" scenarios from circumstances they themselves created. We evoke sympathy strategically, in ways that discourage prying by making others feel bad for feeling suspicious.

How exactly I saw this coming is difficult to pin down. One explanation is that we tend to be highly attuned to the most important aspects of our lives. And when that thing is the mandatory usage of an increasing amount of drugs, taking pains to ensure the continued accomplishment of this malignant mission seems more sensible than extrasensory. As my intake continuously climbed, it didn't take ESP for me to realize I was going to need a more accessible escape hatch in the not-so-distant future.

Against this background, it became more plausible to Patty when, suddenly, it became easier for me to do extra work on Sundays rather than staying late all the time on weeknights. The combination of me being refreshed and the office being quiet, I claimed, made me more efficient. And indeed it did, in a sense.

In addition to allowing me to jam upwards of an eight-ball up my nose, it allowed me to do something acutely substance-specific: incessantly watch porn. As my sprees entailed more and more blow, I became incredibly horny and irredeemably impotent, the infamous cocaine Catch 22. Disgusting details aside, the key takeaway is that my addiction had sprouted another obsession that demanded my isolation from others, especially from my wife.

Tying all this together, albeit barely as my illness progressed, was an addict's ability to convince myself that, so long as I remained hooked on cocaine, this was the best possible of all setups. Consider me the Candide of cokeheads.

In my deteriorating grip on reality, it made sense to separate my addiction from the workweek and from Patty, and snorting myself into oblivion at my office on

Sundays was the ideal way to accomplish this. If I got enough coke in me that day, I reasoned, I'd probably only have to get truly high once more during the week. I could Mad Libs excuse my way through one deep nosedive a week better than I could two. Sundays, I reasoned, got me halfway home each week.

And it worked—until, as is always the case with addiction, it didn't. The minor, intertwined lies told over time set the stage for a grand weekly self-defilement. All this played out over many months. It was somewhere in the vicinity of a year and a half from the time I crossed the line into addiction to the unceremonious dismissal that opened this chapter. I had to create an alternate world for Patty large enough for me to successfully use in the real one. And for a while I did exactly that.

≈

My text message: "Remember my friend Mike from school? He's back in town. Going to meet up with him for dinner and a few drinks tonight."

Patty's reply: K.

Invariably, there were times when addiction demanded quenching without a ready-made execution plan. In such instances, my go-to excuse was to invent a sudden obligation or invitation from a friend Patty barely, if at all, knew from Adam.

This was, simply, the path of least resistance. When you live in the city where you went to college, and when your wife didn't go to that school, a bumper crop of pretend friends can be harvested.

And once I was free, I was...well, just *out there*. An addict unleashed in the biggest city in the country, chatting up dopey people in dingy bars in between generous lines of cocaine in dirty bathrooms. Before it makes you a zombie, coke makes you really chummy, which anyone familiar with my generally antisocial, apathetic self knows is the polar opposite of my normal state.

Texting Patty that we met up with another friend and will be out just a little later than expected. Paying extortionate bodega prices for yet another pack of cigarettes before stumbling into yet another bar, too paranoid to stay in one place too long lest my frequent sojourns to the men's room raise too many eyebrows among my newfound phony friends. And soon enough... numbness. Hopping a cab back to Brooklyn, crawling into bed and back out of it, feigning mild drunkenness when I was actually severely high. Sleepless, heart racing, pretending to watch TV as I blew through the last of the blow, straining for any signs of Patty stirring from the bedroom.

I got away with it plenty of times. Until one night I didn't. One night she caught me red-handed and white-nosed at 2 am, and there wasn't a hell of a lot I could say.

Eventually, the time arrives when a married addict cannot completely hide their addiction from their spouse. The excess drinking and/or drugging either becomes too obvious or, less directly but often just as damning, the addict's actions become so erratic that blanket explanations no longer suffice. At that point, the addict has three options.

The first is to dig the rabbit hole even deeper, devising increasingly outlandish rationales for their oddball behavior. This may be a viable path for some addicts but, as previously stated, Patty is really smart and she now had more than enough evidence that something was seriously amiss.

The second is to spill their guts, tell the truth and make an attempt at getting clean and sober. I simply wasn't ready for that. I wasn't done. This was a blip, not a bottom.

The only other option is strategically trickling just enough truth to satisfy an understandably angry, alarmed spouse without completely disarming themselves. I wasn't ready to close Fantasyland, but knew it had to be restructured to stay in business. Its lone patron, Patty, wasn't buying it anymore.

"I've been having trouble staying away from cocaine when I get drunk," I offered, a half-truth nonetheless more accurate than anything I'd said to Patty in quite some time.

At this point, the marriage has entered the slow-drip phase of one spouse's addiction. The addict's condition has progressed to a point where keeping their spouse completely in the dark simply isn't possible. The first dynamic of this phase, then, is sheer necessity. Leaving Patty certainly suspicious but ultimately unaware of anywhere near the full extent of my drug use was my only means of avoiding more drastic measures—remorse, rehab, recovery—that I was desperate to delay. Addicts will do what they must to keep using, even if it means incriminating themselves.

Ever so slightly, that is. My *mea culpa* fell far short of the unabridged shitshow my secret life had become. And though even this small glimmer of truth was born of desperation, once day broke my addict brain began scheming on how this turn of events could be twisted to deter Patty's further enlightenment on this most important of matters.

Above all, clueing Patty in *just a little* to my troubling relationship with cocaine allowed me to bend timelines. For example, in late 2009 Patty saw the nearly maxed-out balance on the lone credit card I still had solely in my name, a result of me forgetting to close the browser (married addicts generally go paperless when it comes to billing, for obvious reasons). I placated Patty by saying yes, some of that was exactly what she thought it was, but that it was in the past now.

Again, we *want* to give our spouses the benefit of the doubt; in this case, the not-even-half-truth I'd fed my wife benefitted me by allaying her emerging doubts about my wellbeing. Had she known nothing at all about my history with drugs, explaining that away would have been more difficult.

My lingering nasal issues? Remnants of my nostril-polluting past. That rolled up dollar bill with white powder on it you found tucked under the rug? From a while ago, maybe even from that night you caught me at 2 am.

On the game goes, the addict staying a step ahead of their spouse as the circumstantial evidence continues to build and, all the while, the addict's affliction continues to progress. My leverage—once a product of our previously happy history, our dimming yet still-lingering love, and an addict's single-minded motivation—steadily slipped away. Crack after crack appeared in the facade of normalcy, innocence and health I was desperate to maintain.

And then came the deluge: the day when the spouse stops believing their addict partner and starts believing their eyes, ears and common sense. As the truth began to catch up with me and become apparent to Patty, the pendulum of power in our marriage started to swing back toward her. Truth, however awful, is power, and as Patty began to entertain the voices in the back of her head—the ones telling her that something simply wasn't adding up here—a less trusting, more combative dynamic started to take shape.

Addicts can't hide from the truth forever, and neither can their spouses. When one spouse is forced to come to terms with the other's addiction, the truth not only hurts but harms in a manner that threatens the marriage's ability to ever again be a balanced partnership.

If and when recovery takes root, the spouse will need to, as best they can, not take this addiction-fueled deception personally. Accomplishing this feat is imperfect at best, impossible at worst.

But our story isn't there yet. Our marriage's darkest days came first: the protracted period when I was an active addict and my wife damn well knew it.

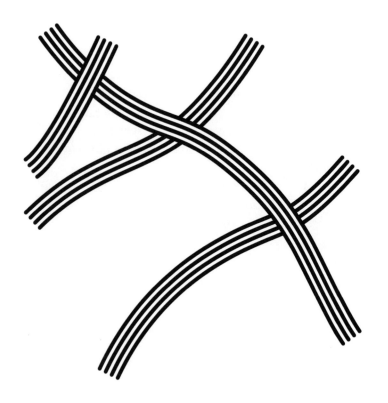

CHAPTER 3:
THE SHIT LIST

This chapter covers a brief but brutal period of 10 months: my dismissal from work until the day Patty finally forced me into inpatient rehab. The former marked the beginning of a steep slide toward my bottom, the latter the start of a slow, slippery climb from its depths. (Though I didn't stay clean following rehab, both the time out and the teaching moments it provided were vital to my drug abuse becoming less frequent and, eventually, completely ceased. More on that period in the next chapter.)

To some, 10 months may not seem like a long time. But for addicts and for their spouses it can represent a near-eternity.

Throughout this book I take pains to reiterate that addiction is a condition with too many variables for a one-size-fits-all prescriptive narrative. Of these, the addict's drug of choice and length of bottom are two factors that vary widely and lead to near-limitless sub-bullets of extenuating circumstances.

In my case, 10 months was the absolute longest that the worst of my alcoholism and cocaine addiction could have gone without one of several things happening, each of which would have made writing this account impossible.

First, hard drugs generally steepen addiction's downward spiral and limit the time of survivable full-blown chronic abuse. Had I never picked up coke, the worst of my alcoholism would have arrived far later and lasted far longer. In this scenario, Patty almost certainly would have left me to salvage the remainder of her youth, and would have been right to do so.

Logistically, cocaine is the priciest drug around, so it shortens the timeline that an unemployed person can continue to feed their growing habit.

Had my preferred drug been opioid painkillers or heroin, I'd simply be dead. Opioids are a more lethal drug than cocaine, so had I imbibed that family of narcotics as voraciously as I did cocaine, I would have overdosed alone in my apartment. Patty would have come home from work to find a corpse one day. That's not an opinion—it's a medical near-certainty.

So considering the cost, chaos and compulsion surrounding high-volume cocaine use, 10 months with no job and a wife gone 12 hours a day is *plenty* of time to bring about an alarmingly low bottom.

And bring it about I did. Unshackled from the constraints of keeping up even the bare minimum of appearances to clients and colleagues, my daily routine typically began around 10 am with a six-pack of beer, swigged deliberately to delay total drunkenness for the inevitable noon-ish journey from Brooklyn into Manhattan to get cocaine.

A few clandestine toots on the subway ride home, back to the apartment to blow lines and watch porn through the afternoon. Rinse and repeat five times, and you've got yourself a fairly representative week in the life of Christopher Dale circa April 2010.

My addiction grew while my resources shrank. I maxed out the remainder of my credit cards and literally blew through the $400 in unemployment funds that arrived each Monday by Wednesday. I pilfered from the joint checking account what little I could considering Patty was increasingly suspicious and, now that our household income had been halved, budget conscious.

The last to go was my 401(k). Nearly a decade later, writing that still makes me cringe, and draws audible gasps when I tell my story even to fellow addicts in AA meetings. I estimate that the monetary cost of my addiction approached $100,000. It was during this ten-month timeframe that nearly half of that debt was incurred.

Here, it is tempting to launch into a lengthy litany of drug-fueled drama—into sordid details about the most intriguingly miserable time of my life and our marriage. And while first-person accounts of addiction's insanity can help the addicts and spouses for whom this book is written empathize and identify, telling war stories for the sake of war stories is mere addict one-upmanship. If you've read this far, I'll assume you're sufficiently convinced that, at my worst, I was indeed a depraved dumpster fire cokehead.

Far more useful are examples of tangible red flags that already-suspicious spouses should see as evidence of their partner's worsening relationship with drugs and/or alcohol.

Often, these red flags are made more vivid by an established trail of breadcrumbs. For example, I had already allowed Patty to peek behind the curtains a bit, a believability's-sake necessity after she caught me blowing lines at 2 am on a weeknight. The ensuing incomplete confession regarding my attraction to cocaine was enough to prevent drastic consequences, but for obvious reasons it left Patty more attentive to other warning signs.

Here are just a few that, combined, left no doubt in Patty's mind that her husband had a desperate substance abuse problem. Spouses of alcoholics and addicts will undoubtedly find many of these familiar. If you're reading this book as a suspicious spouse, they may either validate or alleviate your concerns about your partner. Note that I'm omitting obvious items like missing money, protracted unexplained absenteeism, booze-breath, slurring, white-powdered nostrils or, in the case of opioids, distinctly pinned eyes and slowed speech patterns.

Strategic phone calls. Though alcoholics and addicts certainly specialize in disappearing acts—hours of unreachability buttressed by fake excuses—they also like to triangulate the whereabouts of those likeliest to catch them. Spouses are tops on that list. Generally, married-and-hiding alcoholics and addicts like to pinpoint where their spouses are before getting too drunk (slurred speech) or high (stuffed up or strung out).

This goes doubly if the addict is at home, as I was during my extended unemployment. I would call Patty's office for dubious-at-best reasons, largely to verify that she was still there and therefore a borough and a river away from our Brooklyn apartment.

Easily refuted lies. As addiction progresses, the lies addicts are forced to tell get increasingly sloppy. When Patty came home and asked what I'd like for dinner but I didn't feel like force-feeding myself after an afternoon of appetite-zapping cocaine, I would say that I already ate.

To that, Patty would notice the lack of dirty or recently washed dishes and cookware.

If I'd claimed to have recently taken a shower, why wasn't my towel damp? And if I'd run errands that day, as I'd claimed, why was the car still in the exact same space—a near-impossibility in parking-limited Brooklyn?

Physical changes. These can be more difficult for spouses to recognize than one might think, simply because changes are tougher to notice when you see someone every day. Still, any suspicious spouse should be wary of rapid weight loss, bloating or, if your spouse is typically fit, them becoming unusually out of shape. Skin discoloration (either darker or paler than usual) and a perpetually congested nose can provide hints as well.

But no physical change is more telling than abnormal sweating. Alcohol and opioid dependency cause withdrawal sweating, while cocaine raises the body's temperature while the user is high—the higher the cokehead, the sweatier their brow. On evenings after I'd spent the afternoon powdering my nose, I'd often have to hide this from Patty with a baseball cap, without which the profuse amount of sweat would have been completely inexplicable. Even then, my sudden affinity for caps was less than convincing.

These are the types of verification that built up in Patty's brain. This sort of "proof by a thousand cluelets" leaves spouses certain of their partner's substance abuse problem but without a smoking gun with which to confront their addicted partner. Fantasyland had been burned to the ground but, since Patty had no concrete evidence of my arson, I vociferously refused to even acknowledge the ashes.

The result was a slow slide through the lowlands of addiction. I was already deep in my affliction's grasp, with a wife who had a pretty strong notion of how bad it was but only circumstantial evidence.

The marriage becomes an elongated cat and mouse game. The increasingly desperate addict pulls out all the stops to avoid a no-doubter scenario they know will result in rehab, divorce or both. Meanwhile, the spouse is impacted even more by each lie, petty theft and act of sheer insolence simply for knowing the troubled truth behind each.

For the better part of a year, the avalanche of lies with which I bombarded Patty—lies that she *knew* were lies—combined to translate into one overarching message:

"You are not as important to Chris as cocaine is. You have less value than a hundred-dollar baggie of white powder, less sexual appeal than a porno, and less chance of happiness with each passing day.

"And even worse, you know what's happening here and don't do anything about it. You're either stupid, a coward or both."

This period, featuring an addicted but remorseless Chris and a Patty who knew full well I was full of shit but didn't yet know what to do about it, is where the most damage occurred in our marriage.

The symptoms of addiction were making me a terrible person. That much was clear.

Less clear—and more difficult to admit due to its patent unfairness—is that Patty was also becoming a worse person. My addiction was instilling character defects in her that were previously not part of her being.

This is the hard truth of a marriage impacted by one spouse's alcoholism or drug addiction: the non-addicted spouse *also* becomes a worse person simply for being closest to the carnage. Addiction isn't cancer or multiple sclerosis; it is a sickness of culpability and chaos, one where those nearest the sufferer have scars as deep or deeper than the afflicted person himself and, as we'll see in later chapters, far less recognition or resources to heal those wounds than the alcoholic or addict.

With each new lie, I was making Patty a less mentally sound, good-natured person. I was unraveling the well-put-together woman who had walked down the aisle with me less than five years earlier. I was ruining her current life and dimming her prospects for a happy, healthy future, with or without me in it.

No spouse is spared addiction's permanent wreckage. Let's explore the myriad ways that I, in the throes of my drug-addled insanity, scarred Patty's soul in ways that would impact our marriage well into my recovery—and to some extent, even to this day.

$$\approx$$

Anger

Before we married, Patty—who grew up in an upper-middle class, firmly intact family, graduated with honors from college and was climbing the corporate ladder in New York—was an inherently calm person with very little to get worked up about. Her life had its ups and downs, sure, but she'd never really experienced anything to be truly furious over for any significant stretch of time.

My addiction changed that not only by elevating the level of anger in Patty's life, but also introducing new forms of anger into it. As someone who has struggled with rage issues his entire life, I can attest that not all fury is created equal.

Most obvious was the simmering, seething animosity she held toward me, especially during the 10-month period covered in this chapter. It is the type of brooding, barely under the surface vitriol that results when long-standing suspicions are now open secrets. For nearly a year, an existential threat to our marriage—my addiction—was all too apparent *to* Patty and all too unaddressed *by* Patty. It was confirmed yet unconfronted, a perpetual pain point. Matrimony and acrimony became synonymous to her.

She also developed a stress-centric temper. The normally even-keeled steadiness she exuded both at work and socially began to waver, cracks in a facade under constant strain of worry and disappointment. Over time, her disposition began to turn, transitioning from an easy, introverted-yet-positive outlook into a more jumpy, acerbic demeanor made even more dour because the source of her stress wasn't something she could share with more than a handful of confidants. Stress eats away at us and, over time, beats us down and pisses us off.

Finally, Patty was angry at everything. At her circumstances. At God. At the Universe for allowing this truly awful fate to befall her. For having her happy life hijacked by a husband she loved but, after not even five years of wedlock, no longer recognized. Patty's newfound enmity ran to the core of her being. A "why me?" bitterness turned someone with every reason to celebrate life into something more resembling a nihilist. Had Patty possessed a "Blow up the World" button during this stage of our marriage, she very well may have pressed it.

I caused this. Me. My addiction did this to the person closest to me in the entire world. And if your marriage also has one addict and one normie, similar damage to the innocent spouse undoubtedly occurred (or, if the addict is still active, does and will continue to occur). It's a miracle any of us are still married—and that was only the first item on our shit list.

Envy

Modern life already has enough "keeping up with the Joneses" jealousy to turn the least greedy of us green. Even in its infancy in 2010, with its scrolling inundation of practiced poses in idyllic settings, Facebook already featured enough acquaintances espousing fraudulent bliss that our social media default was set to "less than." Every time we go online we encounter not friends but rather their public relations representatives. We witness carefully contoured avatars telling tall tales of how terrific everyone else's lives are compared with our own.

Now take that tech-driven covetousness and magnify it with reality. Patty's life really was worse than everyone else's. Her day-to-day existence, in fact, was absolutely awful, and it wasn't even her fault. She deserved all the smiles she saw—online and "IRL"—and more. Instead, she got an indefinite injurious grief that she dared not reveal to more than a few close friends.

Further, this was a very bad time for life to fall apart. About a week after I was fired, in March 2010, Patty and I both turned 31. Both practically and comparatively, this is not a good age for a marriage to begin crumbling, let alone free falling. Our group of friends were largely starting families. Their marriages were taking the next step forward in parenthood while ours was taking giant leaps backward.

But even past the customized circumstance of our age, Patty found understandable reasons to be envious of seemingly everyone, regardless of the situation. When her parents took a nice vacation, she wondered if we'd ever do that in our 60s—or ever again, period. When yet another friend got engaged or pregnant, Patty was alternatingly wistful for the romance that once was or pre-mournful of the blessings we'd likely never earn or receive. Even when a companion suffered a hardship—a colleague made a big mistake at work, or a friend lost a close relative—Patty could rightly tell herself that at least they weren't dealing with that while also going through her own personal hell.

Over time, envy pushes past the inward-facing desire of wanting more for ourselves into a darker, more outward-facing realm. It makes us actively root against the continued successes of others, friend and foe alike. There is a "misery loves company" element to envy that makes us worse friends, family members and human beings.

When we bring these feelings on ourselves it is regrettable, but when they are brought upon us by others, as was the case with the miserable existence my addiction had foisted upon Patty, it is unacceptable. By our very addictions, addicts make our spouses envious people simply by wishing they could change places with someone, *anyone*, to escape their daily indignities.

Cynicism

A kissing cousin of anger, cynicism can be defined as "distrusting or disparaging the motives of others; bitterly or sneeringly distrustful, contemptuous, or pessimistic."

Sounds about right for someone married to an ever more deceitful, selfish and see-through addict.

To be clear, Patty's emerging cynicism—another trait she'd never shown prior to my descent into addiction—ran deeper than her interactions with me. After all, anybody fully trusting of someone they know to be an active addict is simply being naive. Patty's distrust of me wasn't cynical; it was common sense.

No, Patty's cynicism was measured in her reaction to everything else. To friends, to family, to life. Convinced she'd allowed her addict husband to put one over on her for far too long, Patty was plagued by the nagging notion that perhaps she'd been wrong about the intentions of others as well.

Maybe the niceties of long-standing friends were primrose paths designed to keep her at an emotional arm's length. And maybe the kudos she regularly received at work were patronizing platitudes to keep her toiling at a fever pitch for less than she was really worth.

The sum of these skepticisms: maybe these people can go fuck themselves. Maybe I'm better off as a friend-less, career-less divorcée.

Shattered self-confidence

But the worst distrust of all, worse than the misgivings Patty developed for everyone and everything around her, was the near-total loss of faith in herself.

To adequately address the utter decimation of Patty's self-confidence that my addiction caused, we must first dispel initial inclinations regarding its origins. Let me be clear: the shattering of Patty's psyche—her ability to believe in herself—had nothing to do with codependency. Let's discuss why.

A dictionary definition of codependency:

> **co·de·pend·en·cy** /ˌkōdə'pendənsē/ (noun)—
> excessive emotional or psychological reliance
> on a partner, typically one who requires
> support on account of an illness or addiction.

The issue here is one of subjectivity. Namely, exactly what constitutes "excessive" is open to differing interpretations. In terms of "leaning in," how far is too far when your spouse is in crisis? At what point does the love-driven obligation and fealty we feel toward our spouses wade into the murky waters of codependency?

My contention is that codependency has experienced an unfortunate mission creep, with some clinicians too comfortable slapping spouses with a one-size-fits-all label.

There is no way to watch the person closest to you in the world crumble in front of your eyes (and lie repeatedly to your ears while doing it) without questioning whether you are, at least partly, culpable. To differing degrees, spouses invariably pull their partners into their messes—especially their biggest messes—and cause them to second-guess their own motives and decision-making.

So here as in the previous chapter, we approach a self-blame scenario that some would argue has shades of codependency. But this is, simply, placing a clinical diagnosis on our natural inclinations, as human beings forged by social constructs, to assume responsibility for the people, places and things in our immediate vicinity.

We are creatures of community who see ourselves, at least partly, as our brothers' keepers. We have a healthy obligation to those in our inner circles and, when they falter, ask ourselves if there's anything we could have done to prevent that negative outcome.

In everyday situations, such inward-centric thinking is healthy. Wondering whether we could have done anything to prevent something injurious from transpiring is a humbling, pro-growth mindset, even when the answer to that question is often no. We honestly want to know if a course correction on our part could diminish the likelihood of a similarly unfortunate result moving forward.

But in a marriage where one spouse is an addict, this instinctual introspection becomes a damaging hindrance. As her addict husband bottomed out, Patty witnessed a collapse so complete and so terrifying that even the slightest inkling of introspection—of asking herself whether she was enabling, exacerbating or elongating this nightmare—cut so deep into Patty's self-confidence as to severely wound it indefinitely.

As we'll discuss further in later chapters, this wasn't codependency. It was *inevitable*. It was the natural responsibility we feel toward those closest to us, magnified by the marital circumstance of that person being *chosen by us*. I wasn't Patty's sibling, a blood relative to whom she was duty bound. I was her husband, someone she selected from a limitless pool of potential life partners to occupy prime real estate in her life, her heart and her long-term plans.

What was someone in Patty's unenviable position circa spring 2010 supposed to do? Dispassionately recognize the situation and lovingly detach from it? The modern-day rush to label those emotionally invested in their addict spouses as codependent disregards the fact that we are humans rather than robots. When it comes to the person we swore to love forever in front of family and friends, thinking at least partially with our hearts rather than our heads is not only forgivable but entirely normal. It just so happens that in this situation, normal behavior leads to deeply undesirable results.

Like it or not, we see our spouses as mirrors. We assess ourselves at least partly on the most important interpersonal decision we will make in our lives: the person we choose to live with, sleep with, potentially procreate with. We see our spouses' affluence (or lack thereof), physical attractiveness (or lack thereof), and good-natured personality (or lack thereof) as reflections of us, at least to some extent. In part, we gauge our lives by our spouses' lives because, like no other person on the planet, their lot in life affects our own.

All this is over-explanation (again in an attempt to segregate this discussion from codependency) of the simple notion that our spouses are bellwethers of sorts. Patty witnessing her husband suffer a protracted, comprehensive and existential-level meltdown—a steady slide that saw me become unfit for work, deeply in debt, bloated and gross, erratic and altogether insane—didn't just make her worry about her life. It made her worry about herself. It made her question her own judgment on all matters, big and small.

Though it certainly isn't a correct thought, it's reasonable for the spouse of an addict to start second-guessing pretty much everything. What poor choices, based on what flawed logic, had brought Patty to this horrible predicament? What misjudgments had she made in her teens and 20s that had led to such misfortune in her early 30s? And what intellectual or character deficiencies had precipitated those misjudgments?

What kind of woman was she to marry a man like me? She had seemingly made the mistake of all mistakes: she had taken a deceitful, thieving and unrepentant addict as someone worth spending the rest of her life with, and just a few short years ago at that.

As a recovering addict, I've come to accept and even welcome the notion that everything I knew before getting sober was either mostly or completely wrong. I had been a deficient person for a long time even before I picked up a drink or a drug, and the drinking and drugging had only deepened the gaping hole in my soul. Given the hard evidence of the wreckage of my past, the idea that I had to deconstruct and then reconstruct my assumptions and perspectives was more than just understandable; it was self-evident. And as luck would have it, the means of doing so was right there in front of me in the form of group-centric, mentor-driven and empathy-driven recovery.

Patty had access to none of this knowledge or grace. She didn't have drugs and alcohol to blame for the creeping feeling that everything she took at face value—her principles, assumptions, expectations—seemed to have led her to this dark place and, therefore, might very well be dead wrong.

Her confidence in her ability to make sound decisions had been uprooted and unmoored. She knew precisely why her life was terrible and getting worse by the day, she just didn't know what, if anything, her role had been in arriving at this untenable destination. Patty was a walking contradiction: she knew why but she didn't know why.

While addicts get stuck in addiction's cycle—binge, remorse, repeat—spouses can get stuck in a mentally crippling lack of self-confidence that leaves them clueless as to how they got here and what to do about it.

And once someone's self-confidence is shattered, it isn't just shattered situationally. My addiction robbed Patty of her self-confidence not only as it pertained to our marriage, but her entire life. She was left to question basically every decision she made over the course of a day, worriedly wondering whether it was the right thing to do or would lead to yet another stinging rebuke or disappointment.

She became a less supportive family member, a less dependable friend. She became someone who second-guessed everything, from the most basic decisions to her motives in already-complex scenarios. Her daily existence was permeated by psychic paralysis.

Patty, who is among the most competent, poised persons I've ever known, was an unmitigated mess on the verge of a nervous breakdown. She did not cause this malignant metamorphosis. I and my addiction did.

≈

Could Patty have benefitted from, say, Al-Anon at this point? Potentially. It's something she briefly tried. However, it's worth realizing that group-centric recovery often requires abject desperation to take root, especially if someone is an introverted non-joiner like Patty. Expecting someone too busy putting out her spouse's four-alarm fires to take her own slowly simmering ailments off the back burner isn't being realistic. Patty's priority was survival rather than self-care.

Combined, these reasons go a long way to showcasing why help for the spouses of addicts isn't nearly as readily available (the desperation factor) or apparent (the recognition of need factor) as for addicts themselves. This is all part of the unfortunate phenomenon of the spouse not knowing what they don't know.

This naivete, coupled with a dearth of obvious resources to better inform her, would continue to haunt Patty for the foreseeable future. In the moment, all the aforementioned character defects penetrated her soul and manifested as a diminished sense of self-awareness.

It's simple, really: Patty was too busy worrying about my tangible decline to notice her own spiritual one. She was too busy combating the endless, ever-worsening detritus of my addiction to fend off her own less urgent but nonetheless mounting maladies.

That is how addicts make their spouses worse people: by jamming their bandwidth with concern for the spiraling addict while their own systems are slowly poisoned by personality defects. The anger, envy, cynicism and diffidence slowly becoming part of Patty's historically positive personality were nothing more than undeserved fallout from overexposure to a drawn-out catastrophe.

And if *that* seems unfair (and it is), try *this* on for size: Though I had caused this damage, it would be up to Patty to repair it. These newfound defects were far easier to imbed in her being than they would be to extract. And though I was guilty of the former, she would have to handle the latter. Only Patty could fix Patty, something she learned the hard way later in our story. When it comes to a dynamic as cruel and complicated as marriage during addiction and recovery, just because something is unfair doesn't make it any less true.

At the time, Patty had more important matters to tend to than accumulating character defects that she didn't even realize she was accumulating. She had a bottoming-out addict of a husband blowing lines in her apartment while she tried to work. She had a big, bloated, impenetrable problem: me.

As the calendar turned to 2011, one thing was clear to Patty: the status quo was neither acceptable nor sustainable. The marriage was on perilously thin ice, and if the daily hell that had become the norm didn't shift soon, she'd have to start thinking seriously about separation.

Shortly after the new year, I finally gave her all the evidence necessary to take a step that should have been taken months, if not years, earlier.

CHAPTER 4:
AN AIR-CONDITIONED
ROOM IN HELL

The night of January 10, 2011, was like far too many other nights during my unemployed, unemployable active addiction. Earlier that day I had procured my usual bag or two of cocaine. With Patty well aware of my addiction by that point, finding time and space to use on the weekends—the days when she didn't leave to work a 10-hour day while worried sick over her deadbeat addict of a spouse—was all but impossible.

January 10 was a Monday, so I would have favored two bags over one, having likely been jonesing most of the weekend. By that point, Patty had confiscated all debit cards and our joint credit card. But I had a credit card account to which she didn't have access and, in anticipation of relinquishing that card to her as well, had a duplicate delivered.

So yes, I probably got two bags that day. After all, it wasn't my money, it was Bank of America's. And if you're desperate enough to take a $100 cash advance at 30 percent interest, you're likely desperate enough to take a $200 one.

I must have gotten a late start that day, because I still had a lot left by the evening rush hour. Patty would be home soon, so the festivities would have to recommence after hours.

At this point, Patty was either doing mental somersaults to twist her brain into at least semi-believing me, or simply delaying another major life disruption until after the busy post-holiday rush died down at the office. Either way, she had partially checked out, a self-willed emotional stunting that, she'd later admit, served as a buffer between her and the untenable reality her homelife had become.

That, or she was just resigned to the inevitable. Leading up to this point, I'd wriggled my way out of inpatient rehab with an addict's agility. Now, we both knew the next time Patty caught me doing coke, I was going in for 28 days, no ifs, ands or lying my butt off.

The power dynamic in our marriage was, at that point, approaching maximum emasculation. Logistically, I was flat broke with no job prospects and no backup plan should I come home following the inevitable next coke run to find the locks changed. My benefactor, the lifeline to a roof over my head, had by necessity become less a wife than a warden.

And now, one more infraction and inmate Dale was being transferred to a far scarier institution, one where booze and bags would be entirely unattainable and I'd have little to do but take a good, hard and (gulp) sober look at myself.

No couple can stay married in such a compromised condition for very long. Our relationship was unhealthy, unbearable and unsustainable. Every passing day brought another mental scar that would need to be dealt with for our marriage to ever be restored to some semblance of mutually beneficial normalcy.

This was the landscape leading into that otherwise unextraordinary January night. As usual, I feigned insomnia and snuck out to the living room, fake-watched TV on the lowest-possible volume as I strained to hear any spousal stirring from the bedroom, and went about doing what I'd been doing for 1,000-plus days and counting.

Only on this particular night, I had plans the next day.

A few weeks earlier, a good friend of mine had been arrested for a DUI in Vermont. Irony of ironies, he wasn't an alcoholic then and isn't now; he simply had one too many and made a poor choice in a small town with a strict cop. Later, I would show him and everyone else what a *real* DUI looked like.

My friend's license had been suspended in the state leading up to the hearing, meaning when his day in court came he couldn't drive himself. Who, pray tell, would be available to drive him from the middle of New York City to middle-of-nowhere Vermont on a random Tuesday in January? Why, his hopelessly unemployed friend Chris, of course!

I was scheduled to pick my friend up by around 8 in the morning. Which is difficult to do when you're still doing cocaine at 2 in the morning. It's even harder to do when you're still doing cocaine at 4 in the morning. And by the time you're still doing cocaine at 6 in the morning, as dawn cruelly creeps in, it's basically an impossibility.

That's what it took to get me into rehab: a situation where the odds of getting away with it were nil. In the condition Patty found me in upon waking, I may have been able to get dressed and get out the door. But I couldn't have driven 300 feet, let alone 300 miles. The jig was up. I pulled my paraphernalia out from its hiding spot, plopped it down in front of her face, and curled up on the couch in a fetal position. That was that.

Looking back, it was a relief for both of us. I knew I had zero options left and, with my fate sealed so far as rehab was concerned, my serial scheming—the constant churn of excuses, lies and alibis my addicted brain pumped out—quieted down. I wasn't done fighting addiction and recovery, but I was done fighting rehab.

Patty's relief was more immediate and concrete. This was, in her head, the only logical next step she could possibly take. She couldn't in good conscience kick me out and divorce me without at least being able to say that we, that *she*, first tried inpatient rehab. After all, she did vow to stand by me in sickness and in health.

In the Prologue, I describe Patty's family as "so normal that it's almost weird." Patty's family, of course, includes Patty herself. As a husband, I couldn't have asked for a more rational, logic-driven partner. As a writer, she makes one hell of a test subject.

Patty possesses an almost Vulcan ability to coolly calculate even in the most emotional of circumstances. Even when her Tuesday morning is suddenly disrupted by rolled up dollar bills, near-empty bags with a telltale white powder, and a husband sweating and sobbing on the couch.

So the logical thought running through my logical wife's brain went something like this: "If I ultimately have to leave him, at least I can say I tried rehab first. I owe that to the vow I took, especially since I took it not even five years ago."

Past that, Patty was relieved. For a month or so, she wouldn't have to worry about what the hell I was doing while she toiled away at work. Babysitting duties were about to be officially delegated, if only for a short time.

Three days later, I checked into an inpatient rehab in central New Jersey, where I would remain for 28 days. From a clinical standpoint, it would be the longest I'd gone without cocaine in years, and without booze probably since early high school. From a marital perspective, we had reached about as close to maximum imbalance as possible, with one spouse free, employed and non-addicted and the other none of those three.

The month apart would provide short-term relief, but also add a fresh set of stressors.

≈

Let's examine what inpatient rehab, the proverbial 28 days of Sandra Bullock fame, is intended for and, from a marital aspect, actually accomplishes. The former is a public service announcement, the latter fodder for marriage counseling.

By the time Patty threw me into rehab (to this day, when speaking at AA meetings, I describe it in the passive voice, because if I had had my druthers I would have avoided it at all costs), I was a danger to myself and others. I was hopeless and desperate and angry and afraid and exhausted. I was wound so tight that the prospect of physically harming myself or someone else wasn't very far-fetched.

As far as my drug of choice is concerned, I got very lucky. Had alcohol been my only vice, my condition likely wouldn't have progressed quickly enough to salvage our marriage. The descent would have been more drawn out over a longer plane, and Patty wouldn't have wasted what remained of her youth watching a slow-moving train wreck.

At the darker end of the spectrum, had I preferred heroin or opioids I'd almost certainly be dead. According to the Centers for Disease Control, approximately 100,000 Americans die from drug overdoses each year. Of these, about three-fourths, or 75,000, involve opioid painkillers like Oxycontin, synthetic painkillers such as the uber-lethal fentanyl, and street heroin.

The reason is simple: opiates are more deadly than other commonly used narcotics, including cocaine. It's not hard to overdose from cocaine, but it's *harder*. Cocaine deaths are more commonly associated with wear and tear to the heart or other vital organs due to long-term abuse.

So had I done heroin or opiates as violently focused on oblivion as I had coke, I have very little doubt that Patty would have come home from work one day to find me dead. Instead, I entered rehab with my eyes sunken and septum deviated, but otherwise intact.

A note directly to readers still battling opioids themselves, or to their spouses still struggling with the ugly truth: Don't wait as long as Patty and I did. Heroin and opioids are uniquely lethal. If you think your spouse is still using opiates, force the issue. Get them help and get them into an inpatient facility where they are safe.

The first point of rehab is to save an addict's ass as opposed to his soul. It's a safe haven at the bottom of addiction's perilous pit—an air-conditioned room in hell. I needed to be physically separated from society for an extended period of time. This served not only to flush the drugs out of my system, but also to break the obsession-driven routine of trying to avoid using but failing so miserably. At that point, the only thing that would keep me from cocaine was a total inability to obtain it.

Could I have signed myself out? Of course. But that meant divorce. I knew it meant divorce, and I wasn't willing to get divorced because, first and foremost, divorced meant homeless, or at least its doorstep.

Patty had all the leverage. And any spouse of an active addict who has similar leverage should use it, just like she did. Patty threw me into rehab. Throw your spouse into one as well. You may be saving their life in the process.

Rehab's first function, then, is a much-needed time-out. It's basically the adult equivalent of sitting in the red chair in the corner for 28 days.

Ideally, rehab also provides an introduction to sober living, typically through the 12 Steps of Recovery as practiced in both Alcoholics Anonymous and the derivative yet unaffiliated Narcotics Anonymous. This usually means working the first few steps and, hopefully, continuing this work in recovery groups post-rehab.

Whether you ultimately choose AA or NA to recover, or a separate program, the two most valuable notions an addict takes out of rehab go something like this:

1. I am an addict. I have a mental obsession that drives me to drink or use drugs and, once I imbibe them, I cannot stop. This ailment is incurable, meaning I can never safely drink or use drugs again. The only viable long-term solution is complete abstinence.

2. I can't beat addiction myself. Addiction is a takes-one-to-help-one affliction, which is why I identified with at least some of what my fellow addicts in rehab shared. Whatever program I ultimately

choose to arrest my addiction and move forward in recovery, there must be *some* group-centric organization. If I leave here and get complacent, or try to go it alone, relapse is almost inevitable.

For addicts with spouses at home, the time apart is a much-needed deep breath. From my uncomfortable twin bed with scratchy sheets and a snoring roommate, I could think about Patty outside the context of whether or not she was going to catch me doing coke for the hundredth time. It seemed like ages since thinking of Patty had brought any other emotion except fear. This fear had brought resentment, and this resentment had brought shame at resenting someone who, as insane as I'd become, I knew was a blameless victim of nuptial circumstance.

It was the beginning of rehumanizing my wife again. If that sounds ridiculous, well, addiction is insane. And although I would ultimately relapse almost immediately following rehab, that experience alone was worth the month of bad food and even worse company.

Whether it leads to immediate and permanent recovery, inpatient rehab is a step that absolutely must be tried for couples seeking to salvage their marriage. There are tools and perspectives I was exposed to in rehab that, once sobriety finally did come, I drew upon mightily in early recovery.

≈

For Patty, my stint in rehab was the most worry-free month she'd had in a very long time. As she would later attest, that was a blessing and a curse.

First the good news: When Patty got up in the morning, everything was exactly as she'd left it the night before. She could shower and eat breakfast in peace, gather her thoughts in silence and ride the subway unconcerned to work. Once there, she could concentrate fully on her job for what felt like the first time in forever. She was 100 percent certain her husband wasn't somewhere doing drugs.

When she got home, the apartment wasn't full of smoke and there was nobody to grill about what, if anything, had been accomplished during yet another day of unemployment. She could order takeout, watch TV and rest assured that her phone would not ring in the middle of the night for some ridiculous me-related reason.

The bad news is, well, the same as the good news.

As our primary concern is the marital dynamic, we must acknowledge that Patty's day-to-day life improved markedly once her spouse was removed from it. The single largest cause of stress in her life had been placed in a secure container for a month, out of harm's way and out of her hair. But not out of her mind. Patty felt simultaneously liberated and guilty for feeling unencumbered. She was happy I wasn't there, and sad for feeling happy I wasn't there.

And of course, she was scared about what awaited once this marital vacation—I've called it our unhoneymoon—was over. Would she realize that single life was so instantly better than her hobbled marriage that divorce was the only logical choice? Or would she rededicate herself to her husband's well-being?

The truth for us, and for most couples I know (both divorced and still married), lies somewhere in between. Because even as Day 6 became Day 26 and a ticking time bomb was just a few days from delivery, that I was at least about to complete a full month in rehab gave Patty some modicum of hope. She knew rehab had been the right choice, and now, like most spouses, had a wait-and-see approach to its aftermath.

≈

I was high three days later. If you want a blow by blow account of what that looked like, you can pretty much reread the previous two chapters. More money down the drain, more powder up my nose, more tears of anger, frustration and flat-out sadness on both sides of the marital aisle.

However, compared to my pre-rehab drinking and drugging, it was at least a little bit better. Whereas before stringing together four or five days was a rarity, now I was regularly lasting a week or more between relapses. If that seems like small potatoes, realize that people, when desperate, will point to any progress whatsoever as reason for continued hope.

And besides, it *was* progress. Doing cocaine three or four times in a month is better than doing it 10 or 12. I wasn't clean by any stretch, but I was cleaner. Herein lies another important benefit of rehab: even if the addict doesn't pitch a perfect game afterwards, the score typically gets a little less lopsided. My use was becoming less chronic and more episodic.

Incredibly, I even found a job! In May, three months after leaving rehab and hungover from the previous night's relapse, I nonetheless bullshitted my way into another public relations executive role. In fact, I still hold that role today. And if you're reading this, it means this book got published and I probably have some splainin' to do as far as my colleagues are concerned.

So I used less. But I did use. Fortunately, my time in rehab also helped Patty realize that she could no longer shoulder the burden of my addiction alone. She could not be the only sane person in a two-party relationship. Our tandem canoe was insufficient to travel upstream with one person doing all the paddling. We needed a bigger boat.

Patty's next move was to literally move: she moved us in with my Uncle Steve and Aunt Linda, two of the most kind hearted, understanding and wise people either of us knew. Luckily, they also happened to be my father's brother and his wife, and they had a spare bedroom.

Mentally, Patty knew exactly where she was, and had a good idea where I was. She could see I was sincerely trying to get clean, that I had made some progress—the job certainly helped—but was still at constant risk of relapse. And she knew that if she didn't delegate at least some of the worry over my whereabouts, she might very well choose to revisit the unshackled single life my stint in rehab had previewed.

Not everyone has an Uncle Steve and Aunt Linda. If you do, and you find yourself in a similar situation to where Patty and I were—still hopeful but running low on patience and options—do yourself a favor and be imposing. Tell them you're trying to save your marriage and your spouse's life, and that living with them for a while might just be the only way to do it.

That's not exactly how we ended up as a 30-something married couple living in a relative's spare bedroom, but it's close enough.

Patty had obtained, rent-free, two extra sets of eyes that were completely aware of my addiction and weren't shy about calling bullshit if they suspected something was amiss. She had also gained something equally valuable: time.

No longer concerned with being my sole caretaker, Patty's stress level went from an 11 to...let's say a seven. She could exist at a seven longer than she could at an 11.

I am not a doctor or a licensed therapist. If you were looking for strictly clinical insight, you'd likely have stopped reading by now. What I am, and what Patty is, is experienced. We lived through this. And what I'm telling you is that a trait typically shunned as childish and cowardly saved our marriage. That vice? Good old-fashioned procrastination.

Crucially for the sake of our marriage, Patty could now afford to *not* make a final decision for a while longer. She had bought herself, and our marriage, some breathing room by creating a sort of "rehab light" environment where I was accountable to more people than her and where she had responsible, loving people to confide in and, if necessary, conspire with.

It kept me safer, and her saner.

And finally, it paid off. But not until one last blowout.

≈

October 10, 2011, was Columbus Day. For whatever reason, at the time my company still found celebrating a slave trader who inadvertently discovered the New World worthy of a day off.

So I was off, but Patty was not. That's about as perfect a recipe for disaster as any. Around noon, I went out to "the gym." Two hours later, I was in a familiar spot:

parked on a quiet side street with several 24-ounce cans of cheap beer. I figured I'd be set for a while.

Until I wasn't. Until what basically happened every time I picked up a drink: I wanted cocaine. By then it was late afternoon, and I knew a run into the city was pushing it a bit. (I hadn't been able to establish a coke connection in New Jersey, one of the many circumstances that likely saved our marriage.) Any time I disappeared for more than a few hours, the trifecta of relatives now tracking me became justifiably suspicious.

It didn't matter. I was drunk and needed cocaine, period. I made the call and headed east toward Manhattan.

I had fought the coke urge for longer than usual that day and, as a result, got more drunk than I typically did. As a result, by the time I inevitably bowed to my drug of choice, the idea that I was barreling toward the nation's biggest, most populous city behind the wheel of a motor vehicle was utterly insane.

If I had known that the lukewarm, half-full can of Coors Light in my car's cupholder would be the last drink I'd ever have, I'd have chosen a better beer. Instead, I sideswiped a taxi in the Holland Tunnel, flipped off the poor guy just trying to make a living, and sped off into the streets of Lower Manhattan.

I didn't get far. Chases in congested, narrow-laned metropolises like New York City rarely play out like a Jason Bourne movie. I vaguely remember the officer tapping on my window. I know for sure that there was no need for any sort of sobriety test, since apparently I'd pissed myself.

I spent the night in Lower Manhattan's jail, a wonderfully decrepit building known locally as The Tombs. (Months later, I would clean and repaint some of the same holding cells as part of my debt to society. Apparently NYC's justice system is self-serving, and somewhat ironic, when it comes to community service.)

In the interim, Patty and Uncle Steve drove into Manhattan at 2 in the morning to retrieve my beer-and-piss-soaked car from the NYPD impound. When I finally went before a judge the next evening, exchanging my driver's license for a printout of my charges and initial court date, Patty was waiting.

Addicts, I think, have an instinctive feel for when the absolute, this-is-really-it last straw has arrived. This time I honestly didn't know whether Patty would be sleeping at my aunt and uncle's house that night or, even worse, whether I would be.

The clank of the bars and the look on Patty's face was, finally, what I needed to get sober. Patty was completely fed up, and I was completely scared shitless. The notion that she was going to leave and I was going to prison suddenly was right there, real and within reach.

Fear is not a recommended tool for long-term sobriety. But for short-term sobriety it is absolutely fantastic.

The egotistical addict in me is tempted to say something profound at this point, something befitting the momentous act of finally—FINALLY!—putting down the bottles and bags for what has become more than a decade and counting.

But pivotal, even life-changing occasions are, typically, only revealed as such in hindsight. At that place and time—October 11, 2011, outside a courtroom on Centre Street in New York City—I was out of strikes, out of options and quite possibly out on my ass. I was more frightened than I'd ever been and, this time, the fear lasted longer than my hangover. The consequences had become more than I could bear.

Most significant change is prompted by pain. I was in more pain than I could stand. That's all it took to get started on the most miraculous journey of my life.

But this story isn't about me. It's about us. It's about marriage and the balance required for mutual contentment. And here again, we must settle for anticlimax.

The plain truth is, at that point, the marriage's fate was in Patty's hands alone. She had every reason to throw up her hands, pack her bags and leave for our unoccupied apartment in Brooklyn.

Instead, she threw up her hands, packed a lunch and left for work the next morning. It was the last straw plus one. I'm not sure what would have happened had I relapsed again. I'm not sure Patty knows what would have happened either.

There's no all-encompassing takeaway here, no uniform nuptial rule of thumb to deal with a malady as customized as addiction. Addiction robs sufferers of their sanity, then lets them loose in society, resulting in cascading circumstances as varied as society itself. Ours is not an affliction given to study in controlled settings and, for that reason, no such one-size-fits-all conclusion exists.

To my surprise, Patty stayed. To her far greater surprise, I stayed sober on October 12, 13, 14...

Unknown to us, my drinking and drugging career had ended, and the long, hard work of repairing a completely broken marriage could commence.

The imbalance was total, with Patty alone occupying all moral, financial and even legal high ground. For the marriage to survive, a simultaneous next step was needed that entailed me reclaiming some territory while she, often against her better judgment, slowly ceded it.

The rebalancing act was about to begin. And despite my nascent sobriety, now and for the foreseeable future our marriage would continue along the rockiest of roads.

Part II:
Early Sobriety

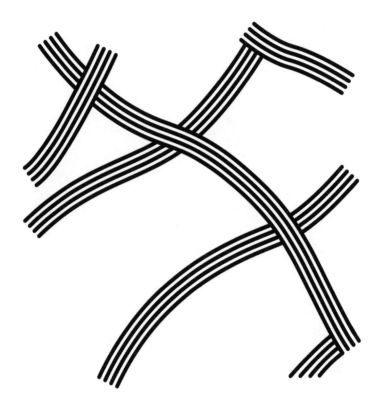

CHAPTER 5:
THE FIRST DAY OF THE
REST OF OUR LIVES

I knew instantly that something was different.

When I woke up on October 12, 2011, I knew I wasn't going to drink or drug for…well…at least a little while.

There's a difference between thinking something and knowing it. Ask any active alcoholic or drug addict at 7:30 am if they plan on drinking or using that day, and they'll say no. This is the truth: the answer reflects what their body and mind are telling them at the start of a fresh, often hungover new day. At that moment, they sincerely do not intend to get intoxicated that day.

But as morning becomes afternoon, the mental obsession aspect of addiction starts to needle and nag and, soon enough, scream and shout. In active addiction, my most vociferous, avowed "never again!" claims were 100 percent sincere in the morning and, with few exceptions, 100 percent wrong by the evening, if not earlier.

On this day, though, I knew that wasn't going to happen. I didn't think I would manage to stay clean and sober on October 12, 2011. I *knew* it.

I knew it not because of some white-light, biblical Saul to Paul conversion. Whether or not anything resembling a god suddenly removed my urge to drink and drug, as some in Alcoholics Anonymous will claim, is as unclear to me as the existence of God, period. I was an abject atheist at the time and, today, have leveled out at a healthy, honest agnosticism.

Deity or no deity, this was a combination of two far more tangible motivators: fear and logistics.

First the fear. As mentioned, I knew—again not thought, but knew—that the previous days' activities had either cost me my marriage or, best case scenario, this was my "final final" chance. As dark as the marital mood had been at various points in my illustrious career as an addict, this was the darkest yet. Even if Patty stuck around this time, my next misstep would instigate an irrevocable fade to black.

For married couples, one partner's active addiction makes each day, without exception, the first day of the end of their lives together. Now, on October 12, 2011, I was faced with the prospect that today was either the first day of the rest of our marriage, or the final day of its inevitable dissolution.

In this do-or-divorce scenario, "logistics" is a fancy way of saying "Besides, even if..." If fear was the fence now separating me—a heretofore helpless addict—from using, logistics played the role of plaster, filling in any gaps between the slats so that the other side was not only inaccessible but invisible.

Because as scared as I was to use again, fear of my progressive self-destruction alone hadn't been enough in the past. Now, my inner dialogue went something like this: "I'm scared to death she's going to leave. And besides, even if she wasn't about to leave, how would I use *and* have any chance of getting away with it?"

With Patty straddling the marital threshold and my driver's license in the loving hands of the New York City Department of Justice, I no longer had a realistic way to drink and drug with *any* expectation of getting away with it. My last marital straw had been drawn, and my last escape hatch, my car, had been rendered immobile.

For me, any hope for consequence-free drinking and drugging had gone the way of the dodo, and the consequences themselves had worsened to the point of unacceptability. It's not that I didn't *want* to drink or drug again—I just *couldn't* without losing far too much. At least Patty, and who knows how many trap doors my bottom may have had from there.

What's my point? My point is WHATEVER WORKS. Whether it's a traditional, sandal-and-toga-clad God zapping an addict's obsession from on high, or a set of circumstances that simply makes continuing with active addiction virtually impossible, the only thing that matters is that an addict finds some path, *any* path, toward complete and sustained abstinence from alcohol and drugs.

This is the first example in a theme that, for couples, is critical: taking a win at face value, regardless of how that victory comes about. The inability or refusal to adequately share joys and appreciate accelerated, often single-sided growth in one partner's newfound recovery bodes poorly for a marriage's survival.

If you're in the same spot as Patty and I were in October 2011, let me first say congratulations. This is the first day of the rest of your lives together.

Now buckle up and brace yourself for a bumpy ride.

≈

Before we continue, it would be irresponsible of me, as a recovering narcotics abuser, to proceed without something akin to a public service announcement. Consider this a word from our (AA) sponsors.

As someone who sponsors fellow addicts in recovery, I consider myself obligated to issue the same initial words of advice and caution I would offer any newcomer. This isn't just an AA thing—it's a one addict to another thing.

For several years, we've been in the midst of an unprecedented emergency of heroin and opioid addiction. As noted in Chapter 4, some 100,000 Americans are dying from drug overdoses each year. According to the Centers for Disease Control, around three-fourths of these fatalities involve opioid painkillers like Oxycontin, synthetic painkillers such as the uber-lethal fentanyl and street heroin. Drugs kill more Americans each year than guns and car accidents combined.

Last chapter I also noted that, had I done heroin as violently focused on oblivion as I did cocaine, I have very little doubt that Patty would have come home from work one day to find me dead.

Why bring all this up again at a time when we're supposed to be discussing the marital aspects of early *sobriety*?

Here's why: because the easiest way to overdose from heroin and opioids is to get completely clean and then relapse. This is because, in active addiction, the body builds up a tolerance to our drug of choice, which is why it takes an ever-increasing amount of that particular substance to get us high.

Once the drugs are flushed from our systems, though, the same amount an addict was accustomed to taking may very well kill them upon relapse.

Heroin and opioids are uniquely talented at killing people who make an honest go at getting clean but relapse. It's simply a more lethal family of drugs that is less forgiving when someone does more than they can handle.

Oh, and if you're a coke addict, like me, kindly be advised that, per the National Center for Health Statistics, cocaine overdoses also have surged in recent years. Most likely, this is because cheaply produced fentanyl—a synthetic opioid 50 to 100 times more potent than heroin—is being used to cut comparably expensive cocaine. So the likelihood of catching a hot dose—a lethal batch—on the streets has jumped significantly in the decade-plus since I've last roamed them.

If you're clean now, I strongly suggest staying that way, because you only get so many chances, both at staying married and staying alive. If this digression saves one person from dying, it was well worth it.

≈

In Alcoholics Anonymous and other group-centric programs, it is commonplace to wish newcomers a "long, slow recovery." The long part signifies that you hope the person stays clean and sober; the slow part is a nod to the grueling grind of fledgling sobriety. Getting clean was the most difficult, painful process of my entire life. But it was also the most remarkable and rewarding.

The same sentiments can be extended to couples. Real marital healing begins only when the addicted partner's drinking and drugging ends. For both parties, as it becomes evident that the addict's current abstinence is more promising than in the past, it is tempting to see this sprouting cessation as an end destination rather than a starting point.

Patty and I looked up, looked around, looked at each other. With cocaine no longer ruining my nasal passages, I could finally breathe in. With her partner no longer ruining her life on a regular basis, Patty could finally breathe out—at least a little, despite understandable lingering worries about my sobriety's staying power.

This is the trick that early sobriety plays on couples: the exhilarating, ecstatic deceit of unrealistic expectations. That this initial happiness is rooted in something real—finally arresting active addiction—makes this spell all the more entrancing.

We told ourselves the hard part was over, as if a married couple who just went through hell had suddenly been whisked to heaven, purgatory be damned. Patty and I were so thankful to have dodged a speeding locomotive that we ignored the tractor trailer bearing down on us.

The locomotive was addiction. The tractor trailer, of course, was reality.

However simple (albeit awful) the marital dynamic during active alcoholism or addiction, the relationship during nascent sobriety becomes, conversely, exceedingly complex. Just as early sobriety is crucial for an addict's chance at long-term recovery, allowing them to build a network of fellow addicts and a foundation of emotional sobriety, this same timeframe is vital to the marriage's long-term survival. Both parties are simultaneously trying to heal fresh wounds, regain some semblance of normalcy and find a workable path forward together.

Often adding to the mixed feelings and confusion is the phenomenon of the early sobriety "honeymoon," an affectionate grace period that many couples, including me and Patty, experience to some degree in very early recovery. We'll cover that in the next chapter—for now, just be cognizant of its existence and wary of its authenticity.

So the marital dynamic of ultra-early sobriety is muddled, messy and, depending on the pull of the honeymoon, more than a little mushy. It becomes unclear what, exactly, each partner can or should do during this tenuous time to solidify or improve the marriage.

Should Patty lean in, attempting to take a proactive role in my recovery? Should she demand a daily download of where I'd been, what I'd done, what I'd learned at that evening's meeting? Or should she mostly tune me out, protecting herself from an historically inevitable letdown and, in doing so, risking a disillusionment that could very well send me back to booze and blow? Though certainly a more hopeful period for spouses of addicts and alcoholics, their partners' early sobriety is also a confusing time frame from a roles and responsibilities standpoint.

Though we now both realize my newfound enthusiasm was due to the aforementioned fear and logistics combo, at the time it was inexplicable to me and incredulous to her. Patty had no idea whether this was real or another elaborate ruse and, because of this, no idea what her reaction should be.

For spouses, this betwixt-and-between confusion is completely normal. In hindsight, I'm finding that our experience mirrors that of many couples in ultra-early recovery. Our result also is typical: ultimately, Patty's paralysis by analysis opened the door for me to decide for her how involved she would initially be in my recovery.

This single-sided approach has its benefits and drawbacks. On one hand, strictly from a recovery standpoint, spouses often inadvertently do more harm than good very early in the sobriety process, simply because they don't have the experience or expertise to properly help. On the other hand—as we'll see in later chapters—a marriage that omits one party from crucial problem-solving often trades one crisis for another.

Confusion aside, what Patty *did* fully understand was that my fledgling sobriety was, simultaneously, emergency and opportunity. This might not have been my last chance at recovery, but it was likely our marriage's last chance at enduring. But again, she didn't know what to *do* with that knowledge.

Amid this chaos trust, or lack thereof, is a huge factor for early recovery couples. This is exceptionally troublesome as, at this point in the relationship, trust is a wholly depleted resource entirely essential for fueling the marriage's repair.

In those first pivotal months, the power dynamic shifted dramatically, despite Patty's understandable reluctance to budge an inch lest I take several yards. After being on the receiving end of years of lying about their addict partners' actions and whereabouts, spouses struggle to believe we will come home at all, let alone come home sober.

The result was an elephant in the room every time I left it. When I was out of sight, I was by no means out of Patty's mind. Though a bit less worried than before, there was a long way to go before Patty would be able to bid me adieu with honest confidence I would return to her safe and sober. The PTSD of a waiting spouse, burned too many times to truly trust, is an excruciatingly slow-mending wound.

That injury is soon joined by insult. Because my wife watched as perfect strangers did something her most fervent efforts could not: get and keep her husband sober. She felt suspicious, scornful and guilty for feeling either. Her downsized role in my recovery seemed unfair given the years wasted playing lead actress in a conjugal tragedy.

For addicts, swallowing pride is a life-and-death prospect pounded into our heads by program literature, AA meetings and sponsors. For their spouses, though, this ego deflation is just as necessary to the survival of their marriage, and generally comes without guidance or reassurances. Considering this, my wife's humility-driven leap of faith was far more impressive than my own. More on that later.

And throughout this, she was forced to cede more and more marital power to a man who, mere months ago, deserved all the trust afforded an asylum patient. The harsh truth was that the marriage had to become big enough for two adults again, and the only way that could happen was for one partner to make room.

This "thanks for sticking around, now shove aside" experience is patently unfair and, I believe, the seismic shift in roles leads many marriages into peril during early recovery. It also inevitably recalls the dreaded C-word. No, not that one—the 12-letter one. Codependency.

In an October 2018 piece for *PsychCentral* titled "Marriage after Sobriety," Darlene Lancer, a licensed marriage and family therapist who has authored several books on codependency, writes:

[T]he longer partners are together, the more their patterns become entrenched. In new sobriety, couples don't really know how to talk to one another. Partners are accustomed to their roles—the addict being unreliable and dependent, and the partner being a super-responsible fixer.

Lancer labels these two married partners Top Dog and Underdog, based on their legacy roles in the relationship leading up to the addicted partner's early recovery:

The Underdog addict is self-centered and irresponsible, and feels vulnerable, needy, and loved only when receiving. Top Dog is other-centered and over-responsible, and feels invulnerable, self-sufficient, and loved only when giving. They both feel sorry for themselves, blame one another, and have guilt and shame, but Underdog feels guilty needing help, and Top Dog feels guilty not giving it.

There is validity to Lancer's description of a classically codependent relationship in one partner's early recovery. Facets of it certainly ring true for what Patty and I experienced.

However, though the marriage dynamic in active addiction and fledgling sobriety may have elements or even textbook examples of codependency, I would argue that the lion's share of couples going through this difficult period are *not* classically codependent. If they were, this book would be pointless. Rigidly clinical, one-size-fits-all assessment would suffice for all scenarios. Anecdotes and personal identification—that reassuring nod of the head that comes with thinking "yeah, it's like that for us too"—would matter little.

The idea that Patty, who by age 30 excelled at a six-figure job and owned an apartment in a nice section of Brooklyn, truly depended financially, emotionally or spiritually on anyone except herself is laughable to anyone who knows her. Patty's problem isn't that she was codependent. Patty's problem was that she really loved her husband.

As a result, she may have *acted* codependent at times, but wasn't *actually* an inherently codependent spouse. Similarly, sometimes honest people lie, generous folks act like selfish jerks and smart people do stupid things. Sometimes shit happens, and real people need to react in the best way they know how. It doesn't "make" them anything.

Life is dirtier than doctor-speak, and humanity is too complicated to be reduced to two types of canines. Patty's reasons for staying were both particular and finite, and I'll bet this is the case for the vast majority of spouses who stayed with their addicted partners.

First, the particulars. Patty and I met in October 1998, both of us sophomores in college. Disregarding a couple of brief, wild oats-sowing timeouts in our early 20s, we were together nine years before marrying. This means that, despite my addictive spiral occurring early in our marriage, it didn't transpire early in our relationship.

No, Patty knew me. And she knew that the crazy cokehead I had become wasn't me. She knew that there was a decent human being in there somewhere, because she knew she was too smart to marry someone who wasn't, at least, a decent human being after dating him for nearly a decade.

She also knew I had potential. Before he completely fell apart, the man she married had been an executive at a well-regarded public relations firm in New York City and, before that, an honors student at New York University's School of Journalism. Upon walking down the aisle in 2007, Patty had every reason to believe an upper-middle-class lifestyle with an intellectual peer awaited.

When that very reasonable expectation started to go sideways, Patty had a reference point. She had a benchmark for how functional I could be if only I were healthy. She had a logical reason to believe that, despite her husband's steadily sinking bottom, his ceiling as a life partner and professional was high.

But always, the debauchery, disgrace and degradation she endured during my addiction had its limits. Her patience with me was finite. The marriage had a red line past which it would no longer exist, a line I touched with all 10 toes before stepping back.

Patty wasn't codependent. She was calculating. Right until the very end of my active addiction, she was weighing my potential against the present state of affairs. And had I drank or drugged after that fateful day in October 2011, she was almost certainly gone.

And if she had gone, she would have *been* gone. It's understandable for someone to procrastinate over such a momentous decision and all that comes with it: telling the family, calling the lawyers, changing the locks. Giving a marriage every last chance at success isn't being codependent; it's being true to the vows you took to love each other in sickness and health, forever. And it's being aware that once the initial steps toward separation are taken, the disruption it causes hastens the momentum toward the finality of signed and served divorce papers.

As for me, my biggest dependency was, well, chemical dependency, and all the batshit bonkers trimmings that come along with it. Labeling a low-bottom addict anything other than a low-bottom addict is a largely worthless endeavor. It's like trying to discern the cause of a car's engine failure...while the car is underwater. You're going to want to dry the thing out before conducting any useful diagnostic tests.

Did I "need" Patty? Of course I did. Throughout my active addiction, I needed Patty at various times for various reasons per various circumstances.

As cocaine went from recreational to requirement, I needed Patty to leave me the fuck alone while I carved out a few hours to get as drunk and high as I wanted. I needed her to believe that I was working late, out with an old friend, watching a movie. I needed to keep her in the dark about the dark passenger my addiction had become.

I also needed her status. I needed a wife, a symbol of normalcy to the outside world, someone who gave cover to the seedier story unfolding under the surface. People raise fewer eyes at married guys, especially when their wives are as stable and altogether normal as Patty. Patty's very presence enabled me. That's not an excuse or a finger point, just a fact.

And as oxymoronic as it may sound considering the distance I'd placed between us, I needed her approval throughout my addiction. I needed her to feel that I was OK, even if that feeling was the result of increasingly far-fetched falsehoods. As my addiction deepened, whatever sliver of reality that remained in my brain told me that the mirror was no place to look for validation. But if Patty thought I was still OK, I must still be OK—or at least OK enough to keep going another day, another week, another month feeding my demons rather than facing them.

Realistically, I also needed her money. Cocaine isn't the deadliest drug out there, but it's probably the most expensive, especially in its traditional powder form. At its peak, my addiction was a $1,000-a-week habit. Unemployment checks, credit card advances and even a cashed-in 401(k) plan couldn't support that level of depredation. There's no easy way to say it: I funneled thousands of dollars from our joint checking account to my drug dealer.

I also needed her roof, her car, her heat and her electricity. God knows I wasn't paying for it. I needed someone to provide for me much the same way a teenager does. I was 30 going on 13.

And at the very end of it, I needed her not to leave. I needed her to give me one last, final-final chance at getting clean and sober. Because had I ultimately destroyed the most intimate relationship of my life, I wouldn't have stopped there. I would have burned through another job, another family member or three or five, and likely ended up homeless.

I needed her to have any real shot at this. If Patty and I had divorced back then, the odds of me being alive and non-incarcerated today are 50/50, tops.

And when she didn't leave, ironically, in early recovery I needed Patty to do the same thing I needed her to do in early addiction. I needed her to give me some space I didn't deserve and some ground I didn't earn.

I needed her to let me begin the long process of becoming an equal with her once again. I needed her to let go of at least some of the 100 percent power she held over our marriage on October 12, 2011. And from there, I would need her to continue letting go not only of power, but her heretofore undisputed claim to our union's moral high ground.

If she were codependent, she would have needed years of therapy and Al-Anon and whatever else to achieve this. But Patty wasn't codependent, and I doubt many of you truly are either. She simply fell into some of the same patterns that nearly all couples fall into when one is an addict. And now, in my early recovery, she simply didn't know what she didn't know, an inexperience-driven aimlessness we'll discuss in subsequent chapters.

Above all, though, Patty faced two overarching challenges inherent to marriage after addiction. First, she would need to choose to love me more than she valued being permanently due an unpayable debt. And second, she would need to recognize the damage my addiction had done to her—an acknowledgement that she had literally become a worse person for the ordeal—and take her own measures to diminish these newfound, undeserved defects.

I'm here to write this because Patty accomplished both of these unenviable tasks. Because she traded in being Top Dog for adopting a rescue dog with the husband she loved, two years into his recovery. And later, for welcoming another family member with him, this one human.

It was not a perfect process. Even as we both slowly healed, each of us frequently veered off course, typically for lack of any clear direction. Fortunately we caught ourselves and each other before the marriage fell too far again. Hopefully, some of what we cover in the next few chapters will help you avoid making the same mistakes we made during my early sobriety.

That my wife and I navigated this turbulent period is among the most gratifying achievements in each of our lives. Here's how we did it.

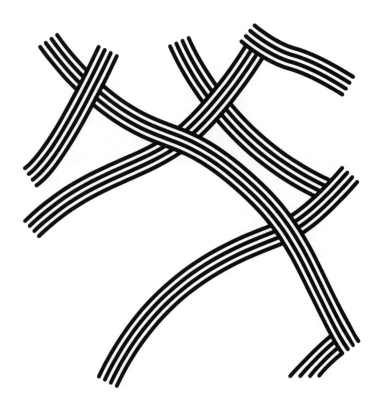

CHAPTER 6:
HE SAID/SHE SAID

"I need to put everything else on hold and just do this."

Upon recognizing that something was finally different, that this time I was desperate and afraid enough to have a chance at stringing together significant sober time, this was how I put it to Patty.

Or at least I think that was how I put it. Remembering exact quotes in ultra-early sobriety is a tall task. I think I said it, or at least something similar. Perhaps I wasn't sober enough to put it so soberly.

Regardless, the dual takeaway is that a) that's what I should have said because, crucially, b) *that's how I felt and acted*. Those were the words that matched my quiet determination to finally get sober, and that reflected my intended course of action for accomplishing this elusive goal. So ideally, but by no means definitely, I said them out loud for Patty to hear.

Aloud or implied, my heart and instincts were in the right place, a rarity in recent years. The sentiment expressed exactly what I, and what anyone in my position, would be well-advised to do: focus nearly exclusively on getting and staying clean and sober.

But to spouses, this sincere commitment to recovery also brings a threat, a layered warning I neither meant to convey nor was Patty able to immediately recognize. My head wasn't clear enough to speak in layers yet, and Patty had long since been trained to disregard my words, however professedly profound.

But a message, even one unintentionally transmitted by the sender and not taken particularly seriously by the recipient, is still a message. And the message neither I nor Patty understood was that for the time being, for me to chase recovery as fervently as I chased cocaine, the "everything else" I would set aside included Patty herself.

Many addiction experts, including the esteemed Darlene Lancer, JD, MFT, whom I excerpted in the previous chapter, describe instances of a "honeymoon period" in early recovery. This is a grace period of sorts, when the newly clean addict and their spouse reaffirm their love and commitment to each other by being on their best behavior, with an eye toward easier times ahead. They are reinvigorated, rededicated to each other, optimistic for the future.

And they really need to snap the hell out of it.

If Patty and I fell into this lovey-dovey trap—and we did—then I believe anyone can. This is because Patty, despite her deep love for me, is both a pragmatist and a skeptic, and because my bottom was so low that my generating good tidings for anything or anyone was a stretch. So we were unlikely candidates for such sudden sentimentality, but nonetheless found ourselves hugging and kissing through wistful tears.

If you find yourselves in early sobriety wedded bliss, I implore you to be smarter than Patty and I were and nip it in the nuptial bud, fast. Because what you're feeling isn't healthy tenderness. It's misdirected fear.

Though subconscious, Patty's fears were twofold. The first and most obvious fear was that I'd relapse yet again, and that if I did, she'd feel obliged to finally heed the increasingly loud voice in her head urging her to leave me. She wouldn't have respected herself much longer had I gone out and she stayed put. Patty was afraid that our entire marriage rested on me getting it right this time—a very reasonable and likely accurate fear.

Patty also was afraid of what me getting clean and sober would mean for our marriage. Her unexpected (and undeserved) burst of affection for me was rooted not in love but *fear of not being loved*. She was frightened at the prospect of me getting better and then rejecting her, worried that a clear-headed Chris wouldn't choose, or rather re-choose, to spend the rest of his life with her.

This is a facet of codependency that nearly all spouses of newly recovering addicts and alcoholics are likely to experience. Such a large part of Patty's life had been tending to my idiocy that she didn't know what a post-idiot Chris really looked like, or how he related to her. Change—even good change—can be unpredictable and therefore unsettling. Again, this doesn't make Patty a codependent wife. It makes her as normal as the next spouse in those most difficult of circumstances.

Back on Lover's Lane, Patty realized none of this. She simply wasn't the type of person to knowingly act a fool. She's too proud a woman and too poor an actress for that.

For my part, I was afraid of, well, pretty much everything. Pinpointing the motivations behind any addict's actions during ultra-early sobriety is at best estimated guesswork, but it's safe to suppose I was deathly afraid of losing Patty and, noticing a newfound amiability in her, was more than happy to return the pleasantries.

It's also probable that, after three-plus years of straining and flat-out ruining relationships, I wasn't going to look a gift horse in the mouth when some real, if ill-advised, kindness was thrown my way. At that point I would have gladly accepted warmth from a serial killer for lack of it elsewhere.

If that sounds nuts, that's because it is, and because I was. As you might have noticed, in this chapter I've used words like "may," "probable" and "estimated guesswork." This is because I honestly don't remember everything from early sobriety (and yes, I realize this complicates the memoir aspect of this narrative).

Early sobriety is a blur reconstructed piece by piece, because the mind of an insane person doesn't instantly clear up simply from a few weeks of physical sobriety. The notion that I was processing information accurately enough to spotlessly recall it more than a decade later is absurd. Any addict who can relay an exacting account of his first days and weeks clean and sober is writing a work of fiction, no "mays," "probables" or "estimated guesswork" about it.

And if that sounded like aimless digression, it wasn't. My severely compromised mental state—which, in hearing the stories of countless alcoholics and addicts over the years, I've come to believe is quite typical—is a key factor in the marital equation.

Patty was operating in fear, while I was operating in a fog. This means that, however well-intended the honeymoon, as far as our marriage was concerned neither of us were operating at a capacity to build anything useful or sustainable. In terms of the marriage, we were looking inward at each other when we should have been looking outward. We were doubling down on each other rather than cooling off from each other.

In Chapter 3 we discussed the abject normalcy of "leaning in" when a spouse is in crisis. Perhaps instinctively, even with the crisis of active addiction suspended, both of us now leaned into this latest marital obstacle rather than what we should have been doing: leaning out.

Granted, even in its erroneous roots, the honeymoon conditions have some degree of value. Sometimes two people who've felt far too miserable for far too long simply need a reason to feel OK for a while.

However, some practical advice would be to make this short. Because one of you—you can guess who—has a hell of a lot of work to do in the short term, and the other also has work to do (more on this in Chapter 7).

All this isn't to say that the renewed affection isn't at least partially real, or even really gratifying. After all, the two of you love each other. It's just saying that it isn't particularly useful. Because this affection, like much of the relationship during active addiction, is a house of cards built on false hope. Expectations are the parents of disappointment, and this reprieve, however welcome, lowers each partner's defenses for the exceedingly difficult task ahead.

Warm fuzzy feelings aside, there are more important things each spouse should be doing than fawning over the other. In fact, that suddenly sappy atmosphere can distract from the urgency of the moment. In early sobriety, time is of the essence, and the recovering addict especially needs to stop doting and start doing.

It is important for the spouse to recognize that they are not a sizable part of the answer. Their freshly sober significant other needs recovery rather than romance or even reconciliation. The spouse's time will come—just not yet, and in the meantime there are other matters to address.

As counterintuitive as it sounds, then, what both partners need at the very beginning of one spouse's journey in recovery is *not* rededication or reconnection to each other. It's the exact opposite: they need space to regain their individual sanity.

Let's look at why this is the case from each spouse's perspective, and explore the unavoidable alienation that results when two people realize their honeymoon period is largely a sham.

≈

Let's start with the recovering addict, whose period of fledgling recovery is the most important time frame in their life. If you have a highlighter handy, might I suggest using it on the previous sentence.

We've already discussed how the early recovery honeymoon has roots in fear and, in earlier chapters, how fear can be a wonderful motivator to make a start in sobriety. But an important thing to remember about fear is that *it wears off*. The fetal-position-level fright that got me to put away the bottles and bags had an expiration date. So while the fear is fresh, the newly sober addict must begin reinforcing it with something more ever-green: solid recovery.

Imagine you're a homeowner whose house was severely damaged in an earthquake. You have loved ones to look after—family who thankfully weren't physically harmed by the devastation but whose emotional scars will be there for years.

You're no newbie to earthquakes, so you realize the likelihood for aftershocks is high, and that an even larger earthquake could strike in the near future. Your house needs a repaired and reinforced foundation, fast.

Ask yourself whether, knowing this, you are going to stand around hugging your family or get to work keeping them safe against future harm?

Addiction is like a natural catastrophe: sudden, violent, uncaring. If you don't build a foundation when it knocks you down, you're doomed to suffer the same results when it returns in full force. Recovering addicts need to fortify themselves for protection against the inevitable: a time when addiction's mental obsession tries yet again to dictate our physical actions.

For me, that fortification came through Alcoholics Anonymous. I understand that AA isn't for everyone. But what I believe *can work* for everyone is some form of disciplined, preferably group-centric approach to progressively building more effective recovery tools. Addiction is a physical malady with deep mental and emotional components, so any effective treatment involves learning skills to both remain sober and address the underlying issues that led us to drink and drug in the first place.

This effort is severely front-loaded, meaning that the ground gained in the first weeks and months of recovery is absolutely critical. Newcomers to AA are instructed to do a "90 in 90"—90 meetings in 90 days, meaning a daily meeting for three months. Other programs have similarly extensive demands for the newly clean and sober. We need to break bad habits and make good ones.

And crucially, we need to identify with fellow recovering addicts. For one, we need to realize that we're not tragically unique cases of addiction. We need a remedy for the so-called "only lonely" syndrome of the alienated addict, and that remedy only comes when we hear from others who drank and drugged as we did: to oblivion. Psychiatry and psychology and medical science in general are useful as ancillary tools, but addiction is a "takes one to help one" affliction. Our primary weapons to combat it are each other.

That being the case, identifying with fellow addicts communicates the most vital message of early sobriety: that longstanding recovery is possible, and that adhering to a program of discipline and self-assessment can be parlayed into freedom from the most vexing problem we've ever faced.

Why I chose AA is simple: it was, and remains, the most widely available program of recovery. But I believe the sought-after result—a strong foundation of recovery—can be built by any number of established group programs.

Regardless of your program, leap in with both feet knowing that time is precious, and that the reward at the end of this profound push is a respite on firmer ground. You only need to get this right once, so get it right *right now*.

Use any and all strength you can muster to start moving forward and keep moving forward. Let your feet lead your head and your head lead your heart. Your mind is racing without alcohol and drugs to shut it up.

Recognize that, try your best not to overthink, and just take the next right action.

Forget multitasking and instead mono-task: do one thing at a time, do it as correctly as you can, and move on to the next thing. Rebuild your self-confidence and self-respect through little successes. Redemption has a snowball effect, so get rolling. But at the same time slow the hell down so that you don't do anything impulsively—in your current frenzied, frazzled state, your impulses will betray you.

If you have any positive qualities left after years of substance abuse, now's the time to lean on them. If your experience is like mine and you don't, might I suggest using to your advantage the fact that you're probably very sick of your own shit by now. Use that sense of being fed up with yourself. Be mad at yourself—not because you deserve it (though you probably do), but because rage-fueled determination is still determination. And right now, you need all the determination you can get.

Simplify your days. If you're lucky enough to still have a job, show up for it and shut up during it. Life is currently more than turbulent enough, so now isn't the time to make waves at work. Pack a lunch, because the fewer times you get up from your desk and walk outside, the lower the likelihood of you walking into a bar or liquor store.

If you have some time to kill after work, I suggest joining a gym. I'm going to go ahead and doubt you're in peak condition right now, so why not add dropping a few pounds to this new self-improvement kick we're on? I was 240 pounds when I first got clean. (The irony of being a fat cocaine addict is not lost on me.) Today I am 50 pounds lighter and have long since decided that I didn't get sober to die of a heart attack or diabetes, nor would I excuse such unhealthiness in my loved ones. More on that in later chapters.

Forfeit your freedoms. If you're one of the many to make this beginning after a DUI, be OK with having either a limited license (many states, including my home state of New Jersey, allow drivers with DUIs to drive strictly to and from work) or none at all. Every time we get behind the wheel, we make a decision, and addicts in early recovery want to make as few decisions as possible. Plan each day out and adhere rigidly to that plan.

And as frequently as humanly possible, get to a meeting or whatever program you're using to combat addiction.

Follow the rules. If your program thrives on sponsor-sponsee relationships, put your hand up and say that you're new and need a sponsor. If you're ashamed, well, too damn bad. You don't have the luxury of shyness right now. And as someone who sponsors newcomers myself, I can honestly say that by asking for help you are also helping us. Again, addiction is a "takes one to help one" disease, and paying it forward helps sober addicts stay sober. We give away what was freely given to us because, at the risk of sounding wistful, we want others to experience the greatest joy we've ever known: solid, longstanding recovery from addiction.

If your program is a 12-Step program, you should (drum roll please) work the 12 Steps. Going to a 12-Step program and not working the 12 Steps is like going to a doctor's office and, upon being called in to see a physician, deciding that you're just fine in the waiting room, thanks.

If AA isn't your thing, let me reassure you that the initial instructions given in the simultaneously praised and pilloried 12 Steps of Recovery are pretty much universal for anyone trying to recover from addiction through any program. I will now explain this seemingly unbelievable statement.

AA's Step 1 reads: "We admitted that we were powerless over alcohol and that our lives had become unmanageable."

If your bottom was in the vicinity of mine, and you still don't think you're powerless over alcohol or drugs, I doubt you've read this far in the book because I've used several multisyllabic words up to now. In other words, you're a moron.

Ditto for the manageability part. Nobody who loves to drink and drug and whose life is manageable suddenly decides to stop drinking and drugging. Also, recalling the primary purpose of this book, the idea that our marriages are by any means manageable—a word that can, in this context, range in definition from "tolerable" to "sustainable"—is just plain absurd. If you truly believe your life is manageable currently, I kindly refer you to the final three words of the preceding paragraph.

Moving on, AA's Step 2: "Came to believe that a power greater than ourselves could restore us to sanity."

Immediately, the atheist I was (and still am on occasion, depending on the day) went to DEFCON 1. I was on high alert against having God shoved down my throat. After all, these AA people were a God-obsessed cult, were they not?

Of course, the step makes no mention of God. It asks me to believe that a power greater than I can help restore me to sanity—in other words, arrest my alcoholism and drug addiction. The simplest answer is that the group of people in an AA meeting, many of whom had five, 10, even 20 years of sobriety, were a power greater than me.

All Step 2 asks is that I trust that their assistance can help me get and stay clean and sober. Any group-centric self-help program would ask something similar of a newcomer. Think about it: if an obese person went to Weight Watchers and didn't believe it would help them lose weight, then they would be doomed to failure from the get-go. So it is with programs focused on arresting addiction.

I could go on—and will, in subsequent chapters—but for now, suffice to say that what seems simple to me at a decade-plus sober was anything but obvious early on. It was a grueling grind that took all the dedication and energy I could garner.

Because all the while, a person in early sobriety is dealing with one set of circumstances over all others: feeling their feelings without feeling their way to a bar. Or, more aptly for me, dealing with my feelings without feeling my way to my dealer.

But again, we only need to get this right once. And this time, I had a fear- and shame-fueled, angry determination that allowed me to put at least some of those feelings of hurt on the shelf. I somehow knew that, had I felt everything right away, the inundation would have been overwhelming. I'd done too much damage to address all of it all at once.

And even with this semi-roboticism—this uber-disciplined autopilot in which I operated during ultra-early sobriety—the gut-shot shame was sudden and savage. It was a physical reaction, a stomach spasm akin to a man bracing to be kicked in the abdomen. The associated thoughts were those of countless regretful moments in active addiction, all with the same voiceover: "I can't believe I did *that*."

As you may have noticed, Patty hasn't made a cameo in quite some time. The reason is simple: this didn't involve her. This was purely personal. But here, the individual becomes marital, because if I didn't get my act together the marriage wasn't going to last.

During this period, the best thing the recovering addict does for the marriage is stop making it worse. Before a bleeding open wound can heal, a tourniquet must be applied.

For Patty the result was...what exactly? As touched upon in the last chapter, she didn't know quite what to make of the situation. Let's explore ultra-early sobriety from the spouse's perspective.

≈

"I guess just keep doing what you're doing."

It was, really, the only logical thing for a person as logical as Patty to say. The feeling she had was akin to a high school dropout watching their child make the dean's list in college: happy with the results thus far, but completely ill-equipped to explain how those results came about.

Patty was in the beginning stages of watching a loved one who until very recently was almost completely dependent on her expand his world beyond her grasp. Compounding this inherently intimidating prospect was that my "schooling" was so foreign as to practically constitute another language.

It's impossible to overemphasize my belief that addiction is a "takes one to know one" condition. So while

Patty, a Rutgers honors graduate whose career involves digesting reams of complex, often doctorate-level subject matter, could easily understand the terms and texts of my sober education, as a non-addict she had no deeper connection with them. She understood the value in the lessons I was learning, and comprehended the messages Bill Wilson so expertly espouses in *Alcoholics Anonymous* (the text that gave the organization its name, also called *The Big Book*), but they didn't resonate with her on any profound level.

Here again, Patty serves as an apt constant in any early sobriety marital experiment, this time due to her high level of intellect. It's safe to say that exactly none of what I was learning in early recovery could, academically, get over her head. But nor could it get into her heart.

Were Patty some classic codependent stereotype, she would have exhausted herself trying to match my zeal for—or at least my understanding of—whatever it was that seemed to be finally helping her husband start to recover. She would have insisted on playing an outsized role in a play in which she'd become an extra. But she didn't, because she knew that her deficit in this matter wasn't intellectual but rather experiential and emotional.

While the concepts and lessons of early sobriety delivered welcome news for Patty, they were nothing short of lifesaving for me. A loved one watching a drowning man find a life preserver undoubtedly feels joyous, but not as joyous as finding a life preserver does to the guy who almost drowned.

For spouses who've spent long years trying to fix a broken situation, this newfound powerlessness can be a conflicting and confounding emotional hodgepodge. Happiness haunted by newfound fears. Relief tainted with subtle alienation. Gratitude marred with envy that the progress their addict spouses are finally making is largely being made without their help. And overshadowing everything, suspicion that this could all come crashing down.

Not surprisingly, these erratic emotions can result in erratic behavior.

The aforementioned honeymoon period is part of these dizzying new dimensions. Though we've discussed how, for the spouses of addicts, much of this mushiness is misdirected fear, there are, I believe, at least some authentic elements at play.

From Patty's perspective, the fact that it was possible to get to this hopeful point, one with even the slightest sliver of sobriety on my part, was a much-needed reprieve and boost. That this glimmer of hope translated into exaggerated (and for her wildly out of character) niceties toward me is both understandable and human. Here again we approach the blurred line between the clinical-speak of codependency and the plain and simple love that a wife has for her husband. To what degree Patty was rooted in me rather than merely rooting for me is impossible to determine and, I would argue, entirely unimportant.

Regardless, it understandably stunned Patty when, in short order, she realized she was rooting from the bleachers rather than the dugout. As vested an interest as she had in the game, she realized she had little real impact on its outcome.

What exactly was I learning in these meetings, anyway? And from whom? A bunch of former drunks and junkies? Addiction is the one illness where the addict's closest loved ones are mostly cut off from the treatment plan. There were no bedside doctors to co-consult with, no prescriptions to help ensure the patient follow.

She was a spectator rather than a participant; and in fact, she was barely that. The idea of her calling my sponsor for an update was entirely anathema to the confidentiality required for addicts and alcoholics to identify with each other, and slowly heal in the process. Addiction is an ailment fought behind closed doors, with the understanding that what goes on in AA stays in AA. Similar concepts of anonymity are ingrained in other group-centric recovery programs.

So Patty had only a partial view of my sobriety—the part that I presented to her. And as history had shown, I was a goddamned liar.

Despite whatever sober honeymoon transpired, Patty's guard was still very much up throughout my early sobriety. Like the vast majority of spouses in her situation, she'd seen too many false starts to believe the winning drive had finally begun. How, then, did she refrain from the unbearable and completely natural urge to act as referee?

Despite every instinct telling her to jump in and demand to know what the hell was going on with me, Patty managed to tiptoe the sidelines and monitor the game as best she could without calling the plays. She admits that it took all the stoicism she could muster.

It also took an assist from what Patty also admits is perhaps her most glaring character defect: procrastination.

Like the addict, the spouse only needs to get early sobriety right once. And the way Patty got it right (or at least right *enough*), the way she managed to muddle along without meddling, was a perfect storm of having the bravery to stay uninvolved and simply freezing up for lack of any alternative solution.

Here again, we return to the theme of WHATEVER WORKS. Whatever mix of assets and liabilities that gets the job done in early sobriety is absolutely wonderful. Take a win for what it is and continue to move forward together. Even, as in this case, when that means moving forward separately, albeit temporarily.

That Patty gave me the space to get sober, without sufficient insight into my methods or consultation with my co-conspirators, impresses me more than the fact that I was finally able to get my act together and make a beginning in recovery. With everything on the line, Patty bit her tongue and held her breath while her husband walked out the door most evenings into a stranger's car, to go to a "meeting." How opportunistically non-specific of me.

While I was undergoing the most gratifying and satisfying experience of my life, Patty was a nervous wreck, clinging to hope against all previous history and, perhaps, even all common sense. Maybe she should have done more than dip her toe in Al-Anon, or tried therapy. She did not (more on why in the next chapter). She stuck it out the way she'd stuck out my active addiction: lonesome, with a major assist from loving family like my aunt and uncle.

I was getting better, she was getting...not worse. One day at a time, she was doing all that spouses of addicts in early recovery can really do when it comes to their partners: hang in there, despite being uninformed and unconvinced.

That's how someone as smart and often profound as Patty was reduced to "I guess just keep doing what you're doing." She, and the spouses of addicts everywhere, could do very little to boost her partner's chance at sobriety. She would wait, watch and worry.

And in her preoccupation, she unknowingly ignored something that, while by no means an emergency, certainly required attention: herself.

CHAPTER 7:
"I DO-OVER"

"I...I really don't know..."

The phrase at once trailed off tepidly and landed like a thud in my ear. It hung there, neither added to by her nor responded to by me. It was the perfect microcosm for the frustrating, confusing mess our relationship had become in the 18 months since I'd gotten clean and sober.

Three hours earlier, Patty had called me and said she was leaving work shortly and would be picking up dinner on her way home. The commute from her East Midtown office to our suburban New Jersey home typically took about an hour. So accounting for the food order I had expected her home in about 90 minutes.

I waited. And waited. And starved. I have a penchant for getting hangry.

At the two-hour mark I called her. Straight to voicemail.

Half an hour later I dialed again. Straight to voicemail. In Patty's defense, to this day she has the cell phone reachability of an octogenarian.

Finally, three hours after Patty told me she was leaving work, I reached her. Was she close?

"No, I'm still in the city," she said. Something was off in her voice. It was simultaneously detached and uncaring yet adrift and concerned.

"O-kaaaay," I intoned, sarcastically. "Why?"

She didn't know. And what was really alarming was that I knew she wasn't lying.

Instead of coming home to her hungry husband, Patty had spent the last few hours wandering around New York, intentionally getting lost in a city whose trademark grid makes doing so exceedingly difficult. First subconsciously and now physically, Patty was avoiding me.

This would have been a concerning scenario for any couple but, per the biographical info shared in the preceding chapters, even more so here. Patty simply didn't do stuff like this. She is among the most straightforward, direct-intentioned persons I've ever known. Going MIA was totally out of her MO.

Something was obviously really wrong with us. Where had we gone astray?

≈

I am finding that the most rewarding part of writing this book is the potential for other couples to learn from, and therefore not make, the marital mistakes Patty and I made. There is a "do as I say not as I do" element to recovery in general, one that leverages the excruciating experiences of fellow sufferers to help those following in our footsteps avoid similar pitfalls.

Since their symptoms are played out in real-world chaos, as illnesses addiction and alcoholism are particularly confounding, and prey on their victims' bedevilment. To combat this, those of us in recovery attempt to chart paths to success for others taking the journey after us, even if that map could only be drawn after several wrong turns.

As exemplified by Patty's belated audition for *Home Alone 2: Lost in New York*, something was seriously amiss in our relationship. Worse, the red flag it waved was as head-scratching as it was eye-opening. Neither of us had anything approaching a comprehensive explanation for *why* we were going through whatever the hell this was.

Patty's extended tour of Manhattan was a cry for help but, like an infant in meltdown mode, neither she nor I could identify the pain point.

On paper, we were all good. In the 18 months since my last drink, irrefutable progress had been made. I had held and solidified my professional position. We had purchased and moved into a home in suburban New Jersey. And following a probationary period in which my car would start only after a breathalyzer, my non-state-supervised driving privileges had been restored (like a big boy!). Of course, this was only after I'd paid thousands in fines and court fees, spent 40 hours cleaning the same Manhattan jail cells I'd inhabited back in October 2011 and, of course, shelled out another grand for the aforementioned breathalyzer installation, servicing and eventual removal. Don't drink and drive, folks. It can cost both lives and a hell of a lot of money.

In any event, logistically we were shedding the encumbrances of my addiction and, approaching our mid-30s, making up for some lost time. A house with two cars in the driveway, check. Two decent incomes, check. Rescue dog, coming soon to a pee-pad near you.

Best of all, I had worked all 12 Steps of Alcoholics Anonymous (again, like a big boy!), and had even started to sponsor someone. We were both confident that I was in no danger of imminent relapse, and we were both right. I had arrested cocaine addiction and alcoholism, leveraging my fear-filled bottom as motivation to reclaim my life.

My mental obsession to drink and drug was gone. Serious thoughts of using were fleeting and frightening, as they should be. I had won the most dangerous fight of my life, and I was proud of that. We both were.

But the problem wasn't me. And it wasn't really Patty. It was *us*. And the solution here wasn't linear, wasn't "do this with honesty and hard work and you'll be rewarded." This was much more opaque.

We didn't know what we didn't know. And what we didn't know was one fundamental truth of a marriage during one spouse's early recovery from addiction. Highlighters out, please: It's never going to be the same relationship again, and you're either getting remarried or you're not.

Fighting that notion is useless. And not being *aware* of it was the intangible thing that had led us to Patty's three-hour tour of Midtown. The inability to realize or accept this fact is the reason, I believe, that so many marriages fail in early sobriety, why Patty and I clashed so fiercely during this timeframe, and why this book is dedicating the lion's share of its chapters to early recovery.

If there's one mistake we made that you're able to avoid, make it this one. Let's look at why this is so perplexing and so important.

≈

I just made what accredited experts in two well-trodden fields—addiction and marriage—would call an unsubstantiated claim. So let's give it some substance.

Let's start by revisiting the discussion started in Chapter 3: in a marriage, one partner's addiction makes both partners worse people. To recap:

At first pass, this seems like a difficult concept to swallow. The addict's rap sheet of lies, petty theft and manipulation is by now well-documented. But the statement's unpalatability comes in acknowledging that exactly nothing about my addiction was Patty's fault. However, being innocent and being unaffected are two very different conditions.

During the three years I spent manipulating Patty's reality with elaborate, often layered lies while robbing her of both sanity and cash, how on Earth could she *not* have been negatively affected? To varying degrees, my actions caused Patty to become jaded, cynical, suspicious, cold. It had warped her confidence in herself to determine what was real and what wasn't, and made her resentful over having been stripped of this compass. And it had made her obsessively question her decision-making, because when you don't know what to believe, it is exceedingly difficult to believe in yourself.

So no, her utter innocence aside, Patty wasn't as good a person in October 2011 as she was before my addiction hijacked first my life and, gradually, our lives together.

To complicate matters, everyone in Patty's orbit had been showering her with praise, understandably telling her what a saint she'd been for sticking with me through everything, and remarking on how happy she must be to have all this seemingly behind her.

However well-intended and well-deserved, such reassurances only reinforced what Patty already knew: none of this was her fault, and she deserved credit for helping steer both of us through to the other side.

And here's the kicker: that all this was rooted in plainly evident facts only made this mindset more dangerous.

The following statement can only be made from the lofty luxury of a hindsight in which Patty and I have settled such issues: Instead of standing still, understandably content with her exhaustive efforts leading up to October 2011, Patty needed to heal in the strictest sense of the word.

Understand how difficult this is for the spouse in this situation. Patty's guard was still very much up during my early sobriety, and she spent much of her time worrying about where I was, who I was with and what I was doing. Personal growth doesn't come easy when you're preoccupied with someone else and, historically, the spouses of addicts and alcoholics in fledgling sobriety have good reason to worry.

Meanwhile, getting better was precisely what I was doing. In early sobriety—especially for low bottoms like me—the incline of personal growth is steeper than at any other time in recovery. This is out of sheer necessity because, as discussed in Chapters 5 and 6, the period in which a person can stay clean and sober from fear and shame alone has an expiration date.

It is during this condensed time frame that an addict must construct a foundation of recovery strong enough to endure life as a clean, sober, responsible adult. And in October 2011, I espoused none of the final four words of the preceding sentence.

I needed to grow the hell up, fast. And to be honest yet immodest for just a moment, to my credit I did exactly that. But I did it with a hell of a lot of help from a clear, established and ubiquitous source, namely AA.

It is entirely unfair that, in a marital setting where both parties would be best served by recoveries along two distinct yet parallel tracks (more on that soon), only the addict has the benefit of an all-encompassing program of recovery, such as AA or other group-centric solutions. It's like seeing two wrecked cars and giving only one of them a tow—and it's the one that caused the accident in the first place.

Again, though this narrative is not intended as a commercial for Alcoholics Anonymous, there are elements in the 12 Steps that ring true as valuable tools for anyone attempting to recover, both in body and in character, from alcoholism and addiction. Following are some of the transformative principles I was practicing while Patty, through no real fault of her own, stood comparably pat.

Last chapter I discussed the self-evidence of AA's first two Steps for any addict or alcoholic with a sufficiently painful bottom. The first is a mere admission—obvious to most by the time they realize the necessity of total abstinence—of powerlessness over drugs and alcohol, and that addiction has made life unmanageable. The second is simply looking at the other people in AA or other group-centric program—the folks with five, 10 and 20 years of sobriety—and recognizing that they have a power greater than we've been able to muster; that they've acquired a way of living that has, somehow, restored them to some semblance of sanity.

AA's Step 3, which entails deciding to turn "our will and our lives over to the care of God as we understand Him," is admittedly problematic, in that its themes are not universal to recovery. I could spend three chapters discussing the various reasons this step is so often a sticking point, including the author's religiosity, the long since dispelled myth that belief in an interventionist deity is crucial to recovery through AA (I don't believe in a hands-on god, but don't disparage those who do) and, especially, the preparedness of any newly recovering alcoholic or drug addict to turn their entire existence over to the care of something that, in many cases, they either doesn't believe in or didn't just a short while ago.

Let's just say I, as well as countless others who've achieved an effective, longstanding recovery, half-stepped this instruction that, unfortunately, tends to give newcomers unnecessary spiritual inferiority complexes. (There's nothing quite like being "out-Godded" by someone who, bless their soul, is 100 percent sure that God personally intervened to save their life while leaving the drunk on the next barstool to die in a gutter.)

No, the most important thing Step 3 does is lead to the rest of the Steps. It is here where, I believe, near-universal recovery themes are represented, and tools taught. Briefly:

Steps 4 and 5 deal with taking and divulging (behind closed doors, typically to a sponsor) a personal inventory encompassing our resentments, fears, etc. The goal here is to pinpoint some of the key character defects—anger, alienation, jealousy—that drove us to drink and drug in the first place. Often, these are offshoots of our backgrounds (e.g., a difficult childhood or other personal trauma) or concurrent mental disorders (depression, anxiety, etc.).

It's basically a process that reveals why we're so messed up. It is among the most useful endeavors I have ever undertaken in my life, helping me to identify my more toxic detriments so that I could then work toward diminishing them.

And basically, that's what Steps 6 and 7 ask us to do: commit ourselves to self-improvement, working toward tamping down our character defects and, in theory if never fully in practice, eliminating them. The point is to gradually diminish the rage, fright and social awkwardness that had affected us so terribly we chose to blot them out with drugs and booze. Our active addictions were, more than anything, self-medication. Therefore, a goal of early recovery was recognizing the feelings we were trying to drown out, bringing them to the surface and dealing with them on terra firma.

My biggie was anger. As an AA old-timer put it to me around my five-year sober anniversary: "You had smoke coming out of your ears when you came in here. A lot of us didn't think you'd make it."

In practice, the self-knowledge and commitment to improvement I gained through Steps 4 to 7 helped me, over time, get gradually less angry over similar scenarios. Something would piss me off something awful and, when the anger started to subside, I'd realize how useless my reaction was, even if my outrage was somewhat understandable or justified. And the next time it happened, I'd get just a *little* less steamed. Over the course of more than a decade, and despite taking a step back here and there, today my penchant for anger is a mere fraction of what it was in October 2011.

And once I realized this—once I realized that this *actually worked*—the snowball effect of recovery began gaining momentum. I began applying the tools directed at my outsized anger to my second-tier issues: arrogance, judgmentalism, envy.

Slowly but surely, I was getting better because—and this point is crucial to our marital narrative—*getting better was a prerequisite for staying clean and sober*. If that isn't a universal theme for recovery, I'm not sure what is. People who simply stop drinking and drugging, and don't address the underlying reasons for their years of debauchery and self-destruction, either don't stay sober or, I find, aren't worth knowing.

To keep moving forward, AA then asks that we clean up some of the wreckage in our pasts. In Steps 8 and 9, we create a list of people we've harmed and, after devising an execution strategy with our sponsor, go about making sincere amends with the intention of making up for these wrongs. This serves the dual purpose of repairing many damaged relationships and, especially, beginning the process of assuaging the guilt and embarrassment accrued over years of selfishly drinking and drugging.

Again, universal. The idea that anyone in recovery doesn't have *something* to apologize for and rectify is asinine. And two of the remaining three Steps are just as uncontroversial.

Step 10 is mere maintenance, asking us to continue taking personal inventory and promptly admit when we are wrong. In other words, bring into your daily life the practices and tools of Steps 4 to 9. Duh.

Step 11 is, admittedly, another tricky one: "Sought through prayer and meditation to improve our conscious contact with God as we understood Him, praying only for knowledge of His will for us and the power to carry that out."

Here as in Step 3, we find some ultra-Godiness that, in my opinion, has unfortunately turned AA off to a significant percentage of non-religious alcoholics and addicts. Again, this is not the forum for ecclesiastical debate. Suffice it to say that, for me as for many, this step simply isn't as important as the more tangible self-development suggestions. Nobody in AA demands that we give equal weight to each step and, besides, many of us, myself included, have found one of Step 11's suggestions—meditation—to be both completely unreligious and significantly helpful for our mental well-being. Highly recommend.

Back to universal recovery themes with Step 12: "Having had a spiritual awakening as the result of these steps, we tried to carry this message to alcoholics, and to practice these principles in all our affairs."

A "spiritual awakening," as defined in an appendix to *The Big Book*, does not need to involve God. It is, simply, any personality change conducive to obtaining long-term recovery. The rest of the step just tells us to be honest and caring with other people, addicts and normies alike. Addicts generally can't stay clean by living dirty—another broad, non-organization-specific concept that applies to nearly any recovering alcoholic or drug addict.

Do I deserve some credit for all this? You bet I do. Needing recovery isn't necessarily enough to *accomplish* recovery. I know a lot of dead people who needed recovery.

No, recovery is achieved by people who *want* recovery. Who chase recovery like they chased drugs and alcohol. And I did exactly that. Again, if you do it right you only have to go through the grueling grind of early recovery once and, commendably, I cracked the books, worked the steps and stuck the landing. It is the most significant thing I will ever do in my life, because nothing else in my life would be possible otherwise.

Here is the simplest metaphor imaginable to explain why such prodigious progress is possible in early recovery.

Imagine one day you are 100 percent sure that you are doomed to die miserable and alone.

Then suddenly, you aren't. Providence, something not quite approaching *deus ex machina* but perhaps cut from the same cloth, opened an escape hatch you were dead certain wasn't there just a moment ago.

Considering this, my getting sober wasn't so much miraculous as it was simply a matter of not looking a gift horse in the mouth. Once it became evident that the people in AA had done what I had deemed impossible—successfully arrest alcoholism and addiction and reintegrate into society—I did what I had to do to attain that most unlikely of goals. Replacing hopelessness with hope is the ultimate sail booster. It's as close a thing to magic as I believe exists.

≈

Patty enjoyed no such jolt. No switch had been flipped on in her brain. She had no "change or else" desperation. She found Al-Anon to be a gathering of mostly ridiculous women complaining about their mostly still-drinking and drugging husbands. Not only was Patty's husband no longer actively using (or so he claimed), these people spent most of the time reassuring each other that none of this was their fault or under their control. Patty already knew that. She walked out after ten minutes and never walked back in.

Herein lies a sizable sticking point with Al-Anon: it is an inherently useful program that, though undoubtedly helpful on some level to anyone who commits themselves to it, has an "isn't for everyone" factor. For spouses like Patty, abandoning Al-Anon is more understandable than her husband shunning a parallel group-centric program focusing on addiction itself. The reason is obvious: the newly sober alcoholic or addict *needs* group-centric therapy far more than their spouses need Al-Anon.

Unfortunately, society does a far better job meeting alcoholics and addicts where they are (the gutter) than their spouses (the curb). For addicts, the effort we collectively extend borders on, and sometimes crosses the line into, counterproductive coddling. Posh rehabs nearly indistinguishable from resort spas and blame-free person-first language (in many forums, "person with addiction" has replaced the suddenly triggering "addict") are just two examples of trying to make a necessarily uncomfortable process seem cozy and judgment-free. In my experience, soft recovery leads to sobriety with porous foundations.

By contrast, most spouses are damaged but not desperate enough to seek therapy or group-centric recovery. And of those in this category, a significant subset will be unaware how deep or far-reaching their marital trauma has impacted their personalities. And you can't fix something you don't know is wrong.

Especially for introverts like Patty, the seeming non-necessity of Al-Anon makes the idea of what is essentially group therapy all the less attractive. Were I in Patty's shoes, I highly doubt I would have given Al-Anon any more than a glance, either. So while Al-Anon may indeed be helpful, newly recovering addicts and alcoholics cannot expect their spouses to embrace a program they find both unappealing and, crucially, un*necessary*.

Recovery programs are a subculture, a perspective-bending exercise embraced by the desperate. We alcoholics and addicts are drinking the Kool-Aid because we couldn't stop drinking the beer and whiskey. Expecting the same commitments from our blameless spouses is neither realistic nor reasonable. It's our worldviews that need shifting, not theirs.

Anyway, there Patty was: program-less and therefore directionless, lacking the incredible gift of desperation currently fueling her partner's healing process. Worse, there was precisely nobody telling her that, despite her abject innocence, now would be a good time to work on healing her own wounds while her husband went about his own, addict-specific method of recovery.

Patty didn't know what she didn't know. And what you don't know can indeed hurt you.

Again, let's step away—far away—from assigning Patty with any fault here. When I got sober, a whole lot of people who'd gotten sober before me lent me their experience, their wisdom, their *roadmap to recovery*. I needed to change, and there were clear methods and ample resources with which to do so.

Patty's tools were less abundant and, crucially, less obvious. Could we have gone to marriage counseling? Sure, but neither of us knew how important that was. Should Patty have been in individual therapy? Considering that she was now, as always, highly functional and logical, that didn't seem like a pressing need either.

So Patty did what a lot of spouses do when their partners first get clean and sober: basically a whole lot of nothing.

And validating Patty's stagnancy was, well, *me*. As my sober weeks turned to months and it became likelier to her that—finally!—things were looking more promising this time, Patty began to feel better. Who wouldn't?

But as wonderful as it was to have her spirits lifted by her husband's solid progress, these good tidings only further masked the fact that Patty herself wasn't doing anything to heal her own unique wounds. Feeling better isn't the same as being better.

In a marriage where one partner is working an effective early recovery while the other was never a drunk or addict to begin with, some discrepancy in forward momentum between the two is a given. You'll just have to take it from someone who snorted $100,000 worth of cocaine in three years that few things can duplicate the rapid ascension possible from the deepest depths of addiction's awful grasp.

But in our case, the discrepancy was likely particularly marked. I was making this outsized progress while Patty, for no reason other than not knowing any better, basically stood still. And when someone is gaining on you long enough, eventually they're going to run right up your ass.

Within the construct of marriage, what results is a sudden scale-tipping of a long-established imbalance, one that understandably had the non-addict in the relationship carrying more weight and therefore more influence.

Then one day, that pattern is disrupted. One day Patty nagged me for no reason, or overreacted to something insignificant, or any number of the mini-burdens that married couples place upon one another from time to time. But this time, rather than dead silence, incoherent swearing or a disappearing act, what she received in return was a rational explanation of why she was being a fucking bitc...um, I mean, just a bit unfair.

I don't remember the first time this happened. But it's something bound to happen to any couple who'd followed our precarious pattern in early sobriety to that point. And once it happens once, it tends to happen often because the recovering addict is trying to reclaim ground in the marriage while the other simply refuses to cede it. Here's why.

When your spouse has been so wrong for so long, the first time they are right is jarring. Somewhere in my wife's psyche was the understandable yet unhealthy notion that the one-sided wreckage of our past absolved her of all future wrongdoing. Fights ensued as I argued for the respect I was earning while she clung to a righteousness never requested but reluctantly relinquished. Unilateral disarmament—intramarital or otherwise—is counterin-tuitive and, given my history, potentially unwise.

But it was also inevitable. Because if Patty didn't start budging, at least a little, the marriage would become as unsustainable as it was during my active addiction. Marriages can't survive permanently with that extreme level of imbalance.

In hindsight, of course, expecting Patty to disengage from watching me like a hawk in early sobriety was as unrealistic as it would have been beneficial—to the mar-riage and to each of us individually. After all, had her intel-ligence and hypervigilance not been worthwhile tools to help get us to this point of even fledgling recovery?

Of course they had. And if being nitpicked over non-sense once in a while was part of the price I'd have to pay along the road to recovery, then too bad. That's one way to look at it, and it's certainly a fair way.

But it isn't the best way. Life is unfair. I had created a great big goddamned mess, and I was responsible for cleaning it up.

Only I couldn't clean all of it up, because some of that mess was now ingrained in Patty's character. I had broken something only she could fix. And she wasn't fixing it. And the main reason she wasn't fixing it is because she didn't realize it. My recovery came with an instruction manual. Hers did not.

And like any negative trait, Patty's inability to detach herself from my every move led to additional consequences and missed opportunities. Here, the marital construct during one partner's early recovery from alcoholism and addiction has unfamiliar, even unique characteristics.

Essentially, Patty was watching her husband get exponentially, almost unbelievably better in a condensed period of time, and she knew in her heart of hearts that she had very little to do with it. And as grateful as she was for my well-being, this goodwill was tinged with resentment, powerlessness and fear. Though undoubtedly positive, my snowballing recovery was a sudden, seismic shift in our relationship.

Or was it? Let's remember that Patty, like anyone in her situation, still had her lingering suspicions about the long-term viability of my sobriety. Alcoholics and addicts relapse. So pardon Patty for not pushing all of her emotional chips in the middle and declaring herself all in. No, Patty—stoic, reticent Patty—wasn't ready to go for broke yet emotionally.

The point is that everything in our recent history told Patty to be more observant of my actions than her own. So that's what she kept on doing during my early recovery. It was as understandable as it was unsustainable.

≈

In early recovery, then, it is the spouse that must recognize, accept and ultimately embrace the fact that the relationship will never be the same. For couples, recovery rarely means revisiting exactly the same magic that initially brought two people together. Recovery means reinventing your union rather than recapturing it.

Out of necessity, newly clean and sober addicts who achieve successful recovery realize this very early in the process. Faced with divorce, unemployment or worse, we need to make drastic changes sufficient to accomplish something unprecedented: total abstinence from inebriating substances.

We accept that those changes would irrevocably alter not only ourselves but our relationships. We have to become better people, to diminish the character defects that fueled our addiction. This was easy to know because it was completely evident, and was easy to accept because I absolutely had to accept it. My life depended on it.

By contrast, spouses neither know they must change, nor can they typically swallow this fact on the first offer.

Patty just wanted her goddamned husband back, and the utter reasonability of this implicit request only made everything more frustrating, more perplexing. Patty wanted Classic Chris—2005 Chris. But that Chris was never coming back because, if he did, he'd turn into 2010 Chris all over again. High Chris. Divorced Chris. Dead Chris.

Like it or not, Patty was getting Chris 2.0. Had she accepted that sooner, she may have turned her attention to dealing with the damage my addiction had caused *her*, rather than the damage it had inflicted upon *us*.

Why? Because "us" was morphing, like it or not. It was fluid, nebulous, ill-defined. When one person within a marriage is profoundly changing, the relationship will never be the same. The sooner the other party accepts that, the sooner they can turn their attention to the undeserved yet undeniable negative impact their spouse's addiction has had on them.

Only once *both* spouses undergo some degree of transformation from their Sobriety Day 1 selves can they decide to do what all couples in a recovery setting must: recommit to each other, or don't.

Patty and I didn't need to stay married, we basically needed to get remarried. Two changed people needed to emerge from a dually damaging experience to reconnect under redefined terms of engagement.

More than anything, Patty's meandering Manhattan stroll was a microcosm of the aimlessness she'd felt for some months by that point—an uncertainty that she just couldn't put her finger on and therefore couldn't adequately address.

Fortunately, this confusing episode was a catalyst for us, a flashing red light warning us that something had to change. And testament to her intelligence and insightfulness, Patty began to realize that some of this change had to involve her.

Though our progress from that point was by no means linear, it was a line of demarcation for us, one that commenced Patty addressing issues she would have addressed earlier had she been aware of their urgency.

From that point on we were growing together, even if that risked growing apart.

CHAPTER 8:
NOT SO FAST, ADDICT

Over the last few chapters, we've discussed the dual tracks along which married couples must travel during one spouse's fledgling recovery from alcoholism and drug addiction.

As we've seen, the newly sober addict's path is far more intuitive and guided than that of their counterpart. Though by no means easily executed, the *choice* is easy for addicts and alcoholics hoping to recover: change or else. Typically, this means some sort of group-centric program that both lays out instructions for early recovery and, crucially, involves others who've achieved sobriety in like fashion. The most widespread of these programs, though by no means the only effective ones, are Alcoholics Anonymous and Narcotics Anonymous.

The spouse's path, we've learned, is dramatically less obvious. Al-Anon can be hit or miss, often because its meetings are frequently dominated by those whose significant others are still drinking and drugging. (A recovering acquaintance of mine has dubbed Al-Anon, somewhat aptly despite the misogyny, the "complaining wives club.") Therapy can help, but many times the spouse deems counseling, whether joint or individual, an unnecessary or even mildly insulting suggestion. ("I'm not crazy, my husband is.")

So in early recovery, though the addict's shift is more seismic, any course corrections spouses must make are less defined, less self-evident and less supported. It's a troublesome trifecta, and in Chapter 7 we explored how it negatively impacted Patty's ability to begin mending some of the internal damage that, despite inflicted entirely by me, only she could fix by accruing and applying her own recovery tools.

And we explained how early recovery can be marginalizing for spouses; how, in fledgling sobriety, alcoholics and addicts generally need to move nearly everything else in their lives aside to focus on their nascent recovery—and how "everything else" can include even their long-suffering significant others.

There is sound logic—and proof via results—for all of these factors. But that doesn't make any of them fair, especially to spouses. In my early recovery, Patty had no directions, no mutual-experience-driven support network, no clear next steps. Not only did she have no gauge for measuring progress, she didn't even know she should be making progress, period. Why would she? I had the problem, not her.

In Chapter 7, we covered how Patty's understandable ignorance of the self-improvement she should have been commencing during my early recovery came back to bite her, and our marriage. She was blindfolded and grasping at straws, and what she didn't know hurt us both.

Now, let's explore the lapses I displayed during this period that, had I avoided them, could have prevented the process from being as difficult for Patty. Here again, we will encounter issues that weren't rectified because they weren't recognized. We'll also discuss the tunnel vision that can occur in early sobriety—an eyes on the prize single-mindedness that, though it serves a newly abstinent addict well, can cruelly crop loved ones out of the frame.

Though it certainly had huge upsides, my quiet, narrow-eyed determination was, for Patty, ostracizing and disorienting. Let's look at some of the main marital missteps newly sober alcoholics and addicts may make, and how they might go about avoiding them.

≈

In Chapter 6, we discussed the emotional autopilot on which I operated in very early sobriety—a foggy numbness that, though by no means sustainable, played a key role in drowning out some of the embarrassment, guilt and rage that had helped fuel my addiction. "Had I felt everything right away," I wrote, "the inundation would have been too overwhelming. I'd done too much damage to address all of it all at once."

Especially for those, like me, who had steadily amassed a mountain of wreckage in active addiction, this sort of semi-roboticism can serve newcomers to sobriety well. Most people come into recovery carrying too many problems to address immediately or, especially, simultaneously. This is doubly true considering their current mental state—anguished, angry, altogether lost people suddenly removed from their anesthetizing agents. When we first clean up, we tend to wig out.

Out of necessity, then, we are encouraged to take most of our feelings, 99 percent of which are ill at that point, and place them on a shelf for a while. To avoid the worst-case scenario—physical relapse—we are encouraged to peck away at our sizable problems, resentments and demons little by little rather than swallowing them all at once and choking.

So in early sobriety, I willfully kept many pressing problems on the periphery, so that I could focus on the most important element to eventually dealing with them: physical recovery. I needed to hit pause on my past to have a chance at a future.

But despite their situational usefulness, blinders are just that: blinders. And some parts of the past can't be placed in suspended animation. For married newcomers to sobriety, our spouses are Exhibit A.

Earlier, I claimed that the best thing a newly clean addict can do for their marriage in very early recovery is to stop making it worse. "Before a bleeding open wound can heal," I wrote, "a tourniquet must be applied." And in the context in which I used it, this analogy is apt. In very early recovery, the addict needs to take the first steps toward building a foundation on which they can remain clean and sober indefinitely. These steps are taken almost exclusively in whatever group-centric program they are utilizing to recover from addiction or alcoholism. Everything else is going to get marginalized to some extent, at least temporarily.

But no simple analogy can completely capture the confusing, complicated marital dynamic at this point in one spouse's recovery. So let's expand upon it.

A tourniquet is, by its nature, an emergency apparatus. Its sole function is to save the patient from bleeding out—to prevent a living person from becoming a corpse. Someone in need of a tourniquet isn't in the position to fret about potential side effects of its application. It is vital, paramount, essential.

If your femoral artery is slashed, you either stem the bleeding or perish. You're not going to worry whether the tourniquet, in being tied to its life-saving degree of tautness, damages some tissue in your leg or, perhaps, isn't perfectly sterile and results in an infection.

Though it typically occurs unwittingly, for married couples such a "save my life now, heal my wounds later" ethos is a common early recovery tradeoff. Only it's the spouse, rather than the patient, who suffers the side effects.

Newly dry alcoholics and addicts for whom sobriety sticks—meaning the ones, like me, who successfully continue to long-term recovery—usually get truly inspired, involved and invested in their particular program of recovery. I've described it as the closest thing to magic I've ever experienced. For many of us, the phenomenon is truly unbelievable.

Though powerful enough to be perceived as transcendent, this reaction is wholly rooted in reality. Quite simply, it's the feelings a person experiences when, suddenly, they are not going to die anymore.

Remember, many of us were convinced we were doomed, be it to death or lifelong misery at the enslavement of alcohol and drugs. We were completely hopeless. Then recovery came along and stemmed the bleeding—a secure, ever-tightening tourniquet applied during the intense, desperate first months of recovery. That we were carried away by this incredible turn of fortune is only natural. Even those of us, like me, who were still numb from the depths of active addiction found ourselves some combination of amazed, uplifted and, most of all, relieved.

In short order, we realized that whatever program we were using to recover was working. And given the stakes, we went all in. We followed the strict instructions, heightened involvement and extra efforts of early recovery and, as a direct result, saw steep inclines of progress. Those of us like me who had failed so many times at getting sober saw their best, and perhaps last, chance at getting it right. We seized the moment and squeezed the momentum.

How could there possibly be any downside to this? We were ridding ourselves of what was, by far, the biggest detriment to our health, our usefulness, our standing in society. And as a result, lives intentionally narrowed to focus almost entirely on physical sobriety began to broaden into other walks of life. Those of us with physical or mental health issues were finally seeing results from medicines long rendered ineffective by drugs and alcohol. Those of us who had jobs began performing at them more competently and consistently. And those of us facing a day in court had slips of paper attesting to our sincere attempts at self-improvement.

These tangible gains are terrific, and should not be overlooked. But what also shouldn't be overlooked is the one thing I, and a hell of a lot of others in my position, did indeed overlook: the person most important to me in the entire world.

≈

Amid such prodigious, expeditious gains, it's easy for an alcoholic or addict in early recovery to look at his wife and say "of course I still have her." After all, Patty's once-likely departure was among the reasons I was finally making an honest effort at recovery, right? And now, she was the closest witness to my budding transformation, was she not?

But in granting Patty that well-earned status, I unknowingly took her for granted. After a week of her not walking out the door that mid-October day in 2011, I tucked her away in a safe corner of my mind, tending to the myriad other responsibilities I'd long ignored in active addiction. I attempted to quickly reengage with a life that cocaine first suspended then nearly ended.

This is another one of those hidden trap doors faced by married couples in one spouse's recovery from alcoholism or drug addiction. The types of setbacks that, in addition to causing pain, also cause confusion. One or both of you end up hurt, and neither of you can figure out precisely why.

In this case, I got so swept up in my burgeoning sobriety that I swept Patty under the rug. I was so wrapped up in my own recovery that I was negligent to—and unaware of—the need to tend to our recovery together.

How could I, and so many who have walked in my footsteps, have been so oblivious? I'm not sure I have the answer. But raising the question and drawing awareness to this early recovery marital blind spot is, I hope, service enough.

What I have is, at best, part explanation and part excuse. Again, the awakening recovering addicts and alcoholics can feel in early recovery is unlike anything most non-addicts have experienced, because most people have simply never gone from abject hopelessness to honest-to-goodness hope. And even for non-addicts who *have* undergone such sudden resurrections of soul, generally the terrible thing that caused them to lose hope wasn't their own inability to stop killing themselves.

In other words—and as I'm reiterating due to its importance—alcoholism and addiction are unique ailments whose suffering and recovery each have condition-specific thoughts, feelings and perspectives. In this case, that perspective is a bunch of doomed drunks making a mad dash for the first true window to salvation that cracked open in a long, long time.

The resulting gratitude and devotion our newfound deliverance inspires are key reasons that group-centric recovery organizations often get accused of being cults. AA in particular gets this unsavory label, partly for its traditional emphasis on God. But a bigger reason, in my opinion, is simply because it is the most prolific program and therefore the largest target.

Of course, AA isn't a cult. Cults generally have leaders with ulterior motives: power, money, sexual conquest. Cults use the weakness of followers to swindle or coerce them into something that isn't in their best interests. Cults also rarely let you leave.

So no, AA isn't a cult. But it sure as hell is a clique.

Recovery programs—especially for those in early recovery—are subcultures on steroids. For all the reasons of understandable enthusiasm discussed above, most people who successfully recover have gone through a program overkill period in early sobriety. Like someone with a sweet tooth discovering a new favorite dessert, we gorge ourselves on recovery. We can't believe what we were missing all these years.

Daily meetings, post-meeting diner excursions, group literature study, one-on-one sessions with our sponsors. We make new friends, fill our phones with new numbers, and start new text chains for the impromptu sober support that, we know, can mean the difference between overcoming a craving and succumbing to relapse.

We begin chasing recovery like we chased bottles and bags, and the result is nearly as intoxicating. But while we're benefitting from the tailwinds of our new fellows, our spouses are alone, and standing still.

Given what we've explained about the newly sober addict's journey in early recovery, I believe some degree of spousal neglect is both unavoidable and understandable. Again, addiction—more so than any other affliction—has a "takes one to help one" element that, in my experience, is essential to getting sobriety off the ground. Patty simply wasn't equipped to be a large part of my recovery at that point. I needed something she simply didn't have: experience overcoming addiction.

However, increments matter. I—and too many newly recovering addicts with normie spouses at home—take this inherent ostracization to unfair, unreasonable and entirely unsustainable levels.

Mostly, this is because we are wholly unaware of our nuptial negligence. We don't know what we don't know. We're just a bunch of recovery rookies, trying to do what's right but failing for lack of foresight. Like other spots throughout this book, my aim is to help you avoid this mistake simply by recognizing its existence.

What could I have done differently that would have placed Patty on a better path? Plenty, I'm sure.

For starters, I could have explained the process more, an observation that sounds silly coming from a guy currently writing a detailed book about marriage in various stages of addiction and recovery.

I didn't do this, I believe, for a number of reasons. First, in fledgling sobriety the newly recovering addict or alcoholic can assume, usually correctly, that their spouse is pretty tired of hearing them talk. Patty had been hearing about how I was going to sober up for what seemed like an eternity. Now, I figured, my actions needed to speak for themselves.

And that's true—to a point. But in hindsight, what Patty also could have used were some reassurances as to precisely *why* this time was different.

Our spouses aren't dumb. Despite her completely understandable suspicions that it wouldn't last, Patty noticed fairly early on that this time around something had changed for the better. What she didn't have is any real insight as to *why*. Sometimes actions need the assistance of a few choice words to truly speak volumes. Context matters.

Here, though, we face a chicken-before-the-egg issue: to have provided Patty with adequate reassurances regarding my budding recovery, it would have taken more knowledge of recovery than someone a few months sober can be expected to possess. We hesitate to try to explain something we ourselves don't quite comprehend.

Highlighters out: Newly clean addicts, *it's OK not to know exactly how to explain your sudden sobriety*. But when it comes to our spouses, *we must try*. I didn't, and I was wrong.

What I could and should have said is something along these lines:

"I know you must be wondering when the other shoe is going to drop here. To be honest, I am too. But for some reason, whatever ability AA [or insert your recovery method here] has to help people get and stay sober seems to be rubbing off on me this time.

"Some of the people I'm meeting drank and drugged just like me—some for longer and with even worse consequences. And even though it's the same thing I've been hearing for years, for whatever reason it's actually resonating now. The suggestions and examples they're giving me seem possible, which means I finally believe it's possible to get this right. I've never felt like this before, ever."

Still, though, had I expressed a sentiment similar to this at, say, three months sober, there are still variables I couldn't possibly have foreseen—especially the neglect element. Patty wasn't just feeling left out of the loop, she was feeling left out, period.

Had I been able to assess the situation more holistically—again, a tall task considering my nascent recovery, but hopefully a shortcoming this narrative can rectify for others—what might have helped is something like this:

"You're probably feeling a little bit ostracized by all this, and maybe a little helpless. I can't do much about that right now, because from what I'm learning it takes fellow addicts to help a struggling addict. These folks simply have experience-driven tools that you couldn't possibly be expected to have—and those are the tools that I need right now."

And then, importantly:

"This won't last forever. Early sobriety has a frenzied pace that they assure us calms down eventually. I'm basically learning how to get my life on track so that, soon, I can get my life *back*. So that *we*—you and me—can get *our* lives back."

And yes, I could have exchanged some of those meetings for a few date nights with my wife. I can only speak for AA, but when I first came in I had it beaten into my head to get to as many meetings as humanly possible. We can't fault group-centric recovery organizations for having a singleness of purpose—namely, getting its members sober and keeping them that way—but it would have been helpful had someone placed a marital asterisk in there somewhere.

In my eagerness to gain and grasp sobriety, I failed to recognize that my marriage's recovery was an intricate part of my own. Again, hindsight is 20/20.

What this would have done, at least to some extent, is to ease Patty's mind enough that I wasn't the only thing occupying it. Because as we've learned, what Patty really should have been doing is beginning the process of healing her own wounds—the ones that I inflicted but only she could cure.

I also should have brought her into the process, if only just a bit. Here, another common AA pitfall added to my own obliviousness. In AA, newcomers are typically instructed to do far more absorbing than reacting. In fact, in most AA groups a newcomer can't "qualify"—be a featured speaker discussing their journey through addiction and recovery—until they have at least three months of consecutive sobriety.

There is sound logic to this. Someone can't share their experience, strength and hope unless they have experience, strength and hope. And three months is a reasonable minimum for someone to digest enough of the program to make their story beneficial to others—which is, of course, the gathering's entire point.

Here again, we see parallels between AA/NA and any group-centric recovery program. With a topic as complicated and crucial as addiction and recovery, it's only natural that newcomers are encouraged to open their ears rather than their mouths for a while. Sure, we can share for a few minutes or so, but we're really there to learn how others did it and gain sufficient trust in the process to stick with it.

But again, this singleness of purpose puts duos at a detriment. Patty really could have used some insight into what I was going through. The answer is open meetings, or their equivalent.

I see far too few married newcomers in AA bring their non-addict spouses to open meetings, which are designed, in part, for just that (they also allow for academic analysis of group-centric recovery). Typically, their families' first exposure to group-centric recovery is the three minutes they share when getting their 90-day coin. It's nice, but it's not giving them any real understanding of what their loved one is undertaking. And without understanding, there can be no real reassurance.

I made this mistake too. I figured that if Patty wasn't attracted to Al-Anon, she wouldn't want to attend an AA meeting, either. And of course Patty, like most non-addicts, didn't know enough to even inquire whether she could attend a meeting. The first time she attended one was a year into my sobriety, when I spoke at an open meeting, finally cognizant enough to start making her a co-passenger in my recovery journey.

It was too little, too late. By then, Patty's role as a bewildered bystander in my recovery had already been established. She had already not been doing what she should have been doing—beginning her own recovery to mend her own wounds—for too long and, as a result, only one of us was recovering from my addiction: me.

I can hear the snarky reply from misogynists and feminists alike: "But doesn't Patty have agency? Isn't she an independent woman?" Yes, but she doesn't have clairvoyance. She wasn't not doing what was best for her by choice. She simply didn't know any better, nor can she be expected to have known any better.

Had we known better, Patty would have been attending open meetings with me on a semi-regular basis far earlier in the process—a few weeks rather than many months. She could have been doing exactly what I was doing: listening to someone who'd gotten and remained sober explain the very similar ways they used to drink and drug, and describe in detail how they overcame that obsession through a group-centric program.

And though it wouldn't have changed her life, it could have changed her mind. Namely—and this is important—it could have changed the three most pressing things occupying her mind: my sobriety, my sobriety and my sobriety.

If the addict's program is not AA or NA, this can be accomplished either by an open meeting, if that program has them, or simply by inviting a few fellow recovering addicts to come out to a diner with your spouse once in a while. Inclusion can take many useful forms.

In hindsight, these tips seem obvious, remedial. But in practice, early recovery is so frenzied, strained and downright strange that I rarely see couples strike the right balance of letting the program drive the addict's recovery while providing the spouse enough insight to ease their mind.

In early recovery, though we may no longer be obsessed with drugs and alcohol, our spouses are still obsessed with *us*. Even in this earliest of stages, when we're still clearing out the cobwebs and trying to find our way, married alcoholics and addicts have a responsibility. We must include our spouses enough that their entire lives don't revolve around worrying about us.

I made that mistake. It was selfish and counterproductive, and should not be emulated.

≈

Another common mistake made by addicts and alcoholics comes in the difference between diving into recovery and hiding behind it.

Encouragingly, alcoholism and addiction have become nearly universally recognized as illnesses. For too long, most people didn't see addicts and alcoholics as sick. They just saw them as criminals, or at best just assholes.

Predictably, what has arisen in recent years is overcompensation for this undeserved denigration. A guilty society is trying to make up for its past by being overly generous in the present.

Here's an example. Walk into a theater full of random people, take the stage and proclaim that "Men are smarter than women!" You'd likely be booed and pelted with peanut M&Ms.

However, proclaim that "Women are smarter than men!" and perhaps you'd be cheered, and possibly even offered some peanut M&Ms.

Of course, neither statement is true. Men and women are, on average, of equal intelligence.

The same backlash has entered the recovery lexicon. Addicts and alcoholics are now allowed to wriggle off the hook by claiming they were "just sick." But just because addiction is a sickness doesn't mean the addict isn't completely responsible for their actions, for the nightmarish damage they caused in active drinking and drugging.

For addicts, making excuses for our terrible behavior just because we were under the influence is not acceptable. Someone with cancer who robs a bank doesn't get to blame the tumor. We don't get to blame booze and drugs.

And this isn't just innocuous—just a consequence-free sign of our kinder, gentler times. This is *dangerous*. In foisting our actions onto our addiction rather than hoisting them onto our shoulders, we build roadblocks to true recovery by disowning the underlying shortcomings that fueled our addiction. If I did something out of anger while drunk, letting myself off the hook for the action allows me, by association, to blame the anger on my addicted condition rather than its true genesis: a flaw inside me that *drove* my addiction.

I've seen too many men in early recovery hide behind the American Medical Association when it comes to accepting accountability for their actions. And I've seen too many wives willing to tolerate such scapegoating.

The recognition that addiction is a legitimate sickness doesn't justify being an asshole—whether in active addiction or recovering from it. Alcoholics and drug addicts are both sick *and* entirely responsible for their actions and behaviors. Those concepts are not mutually exclusive. We do not have progressive, incurable, irreversible dementia. We have progressive, incurable, irreversible yet *arrestable* addiction. Our recovery is our choice—as are all the things we chose prior to choosing sobriety.

Addicts should stop feeling sorry for themselves. And spouses should stop overlooking their married partners' transgressions under the misguided excuse of "they were sick." Yes, they were…but the addict was also a hurtful horror show and needs to atone for that, especially to their life partner. There's a fine line—but a wide difference—between being merciful and pitiful.

Passing the buck affects the marital dynamic in two ways. First, the recovering addict or alcoholic is short-changing themselves and, by extension, their entire life in recovery. They are building a house of cards likely to come crashing down on its occupants—innocent spouse included.

More specific to marriage itself, they are taking a sanctimonious, condescending route. No person in the world suffers more from our addiction than our spouses. By placing the incredible amount of pain I caused Patty squarely at the foot of my addiction, I would have cast myself in the role she herself truly deserved: that of the innocent victim.

My fellow alcoholics and drug addicts, we are not the victims. We're the assholes. Assholes with legitimate illnesses, yes, but assholes nonetheless.

And that's OK. We just need to own it, because much like addiction itself, we can't do anything about it until we admit there's a problem. And that problem is *us*.

Gratefully, this was one mistake I largely avoided, if only because my self-esteem was so low in early sobriety that I couldn't have fathomed a scenario where I wasn't a truly terrible person. In the state I was in, exoneration via medical exemption never occurred to me.

The other factor that helped me avoid this error was Patty herself.

We've all seen it by now: the spouse who's convinced that their partner's shocking array of character flaws are all attributable to their addiction. Remove booze or baggies from the equation and, *voila!*, you'd have Prince Charming. They, too, are on a dangerous path. Had Patty thought this way, she would have invalidated her own deep feelings of hurt, whose sole origin was my terrible behavior in active addiction.

Fortunately, the ever-pragmatic Patty was able to conceptually walk and chew gum at the same time. She understood that I was both sick and an asshole. And it kept the blame for her scars on their true origin: me.

Still, understanding who caused the damage isn't the same as fixing the damage. Patty and I fell into too many traps in early recovery, and would need to climb out of them for our marriage to survive my recovery.

CHAPTER 9:
AMENDS ×10
(OR, STEP 9 ON STEROIDS)

"Your program can't solve everything," Patty retorted.

I recall this resentful reply more vividly than whatever I did to incite it. Perhaps I had soberly ignored a pile of dishes, or gushed about how grateful I was to be clean before pissing all over the toilet seat. Whatever it was, it likely involved sanctimoniously projecting my newfound AA wisdom onto a simple task, straightforward situation or unsuspecting person who, addict or not, I deemed mentally or spiritually insufficient. ("Your friend _____ sure could use a program.")

Sometimes the line that snaps you to attention is more memorable than what you were doing to warrant such a wake-up call. Regardless, it's safe to assume that Patty was right.

As my initial fear faded into a sturdier sober foundation, I had been at best overzealous and at worst obnoxious in my attempts to carry my recovery into everyday life. Most addicts and alcoholics are, by our very nature, extremists. We take things, good or bad, too far.

Exemplifying (and, via fresh-faced momentum, exacerbating) this, newcomers in recovery typically don't do subtlety very well. Thankfully, today I have more nuanced, practicable ways to apply my recovery in a fashion that helps others rather than simply annoys them.

Generally speaking, too much program too early in recovery is too much for our spouses. It can have a counterproductive, often eye-rolling effect—and Patty's comment displayed her frustration with my application of AA principles to the minutiae of everyday life. For her, it was sobriety overkill.

It was also hypocritical—and, as I've learned, unfortunately common. Alcoholics and addicts get high and drunk, get desperate and, when they get clean and sober, get enamored with all-things recovery. Grateful at being spared the final insults of addiction—prison, homelessness, death—we strap on our rose-colored glasses and take our nascent (and therefore novice) can-do optimism out into the wider world. We become ambitious ambassadors of the notion that personal progress is not only possible but profound when undertaken determinedly. Armed with little more than a few recovery clichés, losers who couldn't change their spiraling self-destruction just a short while ago suddenly stand ready to change the wider world.

For married recovering addicts, this reinvigoration-inspired arrogance often is punctuated by a big fat blind spot: our partners. Because while I was busy offering everyone and everything my oh-so-seasoned wisdom and advice (solicited or not), I failed to adequately address the person most affected by my illness: my life partner.

By not placing a repaired relationship with Patty near the top of my sober priorities list, I was derelict in my role as both a husband and recovering addict for far too long. And given my experiences in group-centric recovery, I can safely say that this doubly damning mistake is highly common. Recovering addicts tend to get carried away with recovery...so far away that they disregard their loved ones at home, spouses chief among them.

Having stuck by us through the worst of times, our loyal life partners remain on the "not urgent" list during what, for us, has become the best of times. Our pink clouds write rainchecks with unspecified make-up dates. We tuck them away in a corner of our minds and homes, figuring—often rightly—that their support will be there so long as we don't revisit the indignities of active addiction. And unfortunately, this notion's general veracity helps make it particularly detrimental to real marital progress and health.

Why do so many newly recovering addicts take their spouses for granted? Once again the answer is simple: because we don't know any better. And once again, what we don't know can hurt us, and our marriages.

And that brings us to the best-placed of the 12 Steps of Recovery—Step 9: "Made direct amends to such people wherever possible, except when to do so would injure them or others."

Again, I can't stress enough that this book is not a commercial for Alcoholics Anonymous or its sister program, Narcotics Anonymous. However, one tenet of AA that I see as near-universal to a satisfactory recovery is the concept of making amends to those we've harmed. And for married addicts and alcoholics, the word "near" can be removed from the previous sentence.

Recovering addicts have a lengthy list of amends to make to our spouses—a roster that, per the above addiction-turned-arrogance anecdote, by no means ends with Day 1 of sobriety.

Our amends to our spouses must go far beyond fence-mending. It is a process that plays out over weeks and months rather than minutes and hours. Patty isn't a former coworker or casual acquaintance. She is closer than a close friend, and a more intimate part of my family than all other family members, bar none. She is the one person I publicly pledged to love and honor forever.

A clear-eyed, brutally honest living amends is the most important item on the early recovery checklist. It is a load-bearing column in any bridge leading to mutually content long-term recovery together.

Let's examine what amends are, what they aren't, what is required of both parties and the desired result: a "re-marriage." The goal is a renewed union that resides in the facts as they exist now, rather than the gone-forever dynamic before addiction permanently changed each of you and, because of that, your relationship as a couple. Indeed, this seismic shift continues to make waves well after the addict stops drinking and drugging.

≈

Step 9 is strategically positioned. It is toward the end of the list for a reason. Per the preceding chapters, addicts and alcoholics typically need to look inward before they can start looking outward. We must admit powerlessness over drugs and booze, buy into the idea that group-centric recovery can help us finally find a way out, and decide to walk in the right direction indefinitely.

We then must take a hard look at ourselves, ideally bouncing these reflective revelations off others who've walked this difficult road before us. Once we have an informed idea of what drove our active addiction, we can begin tamping down those flaws that fueled our drinking and drugging.

Those are the first seven steps of AA, in a nutshell. Only after some semblance of the above are we in a sane enough position to adequately address the damage we've caused others. Step 9 isn't Step 1 because, if it were, we'd just screw it up and make bad situations worse.

Steps 8 and 9 are linked. They require making a list of people we've harmed (Step 8) and making the necessary amends (Step 9). As intimidating a prospect as this may seem, most amends are easy. By and large, by the time an addict is at this point, their family and close friends have been well aware of their longstanding struggles and now-fledgling success, and are actively rooting for their recovery. For example, a close friend whose car I cracked up while drunk wouldn't even take the money I offered for the body shop bill. He appreciated the offer and just wanted me to keep doing what I was doing. In my experience, this sort of bond-building, happy ending amends is the norm rather than the exception.

As the circle expands outward, amends get more awkward and intimidating. For example, reaching out to a coworker who was professionally impacted by your active addiction several years after the fact is an exercise in pride swallowing. However, in my experience and that of countless others before me, these efforts not only help humble us moving forward but provide closure to harms that had haunted us, often for years. Today, I'm on terrific terms with several colleagues who saw the worst of me leading up to my inglorious dismissal—including the company's president, who undoubtedly gave the execution order.

A recovery mate of mine once described amends as a "sober séance." This rings true and, inevitably, some ghosts of benders past will ultimately be unreceptive to our well-intending exorcisms. There's simply nothing to be done about that; it is we who inflicted harm and we who seek forgiveness, and therefore we who must refrain from resenting someone for continuing to resent us. We can't place expectations on everyone to let bygones be bygones.

Still, we do what we can. Through some social media sleuthing, I learned that one of my seemingly permanently burned bridges does volunteer work with rescue animals, and subsequently made a donation to an organization with which she associates. Forgiven or not, hopefully my misdeeds in the past can benefit someone in the present.

This overview showcases what most early recovery amends encompass: namely, harms inflicted almost exclusively during active alcoholism and addiction. This is perfectly logical, since folks in early recovery typically have lengthy lists of people we wounded, often deeply, while still drinking and drugging. Once we sober up, we largely stop digging those holes deeper and, besides, our screwups in early recovery tend to be nowhere near as egregious as those accrued in active addiction.

Among other complexities, this tendency to focus only on our pre-sobriety actions becomes a detriment to successfully approaching what I see as the most misunderstood of all amends. Unfortunately, this amends is also the most important: the amends a recovering addict makes to their spouse.

As we've seen, an addict makes their spouse—the person they live with, sleep with and are closest to in the world—a worse person while actively drinking and drugging. They harm their partner in ways that must be repaired for the marriage to have long-term success once sobriety is achieved.

But we've also seen that, as far as spouses of addicts and alcoholics are concerned, the damage and confusion don't stop once the bottles and baggies do. Marriage is our most intimate and complicated relationship, and in Chapters 5 through 8 we touched upon factors that affect married couples in early sobriety. Despite being a more promising period than active addiction, this time frame can be highly disruptive as each partner struggles to gain firm footing on a rapidly shifting marital landscape.

For lack of understanding and direction, Patty and I started our journey in recovery on two different pages, a misfire that cost us both additional, likely unnecessary emotional harm. Not until a proper amends was made could we move forward together as anything resembling a healthy couple.

We'd each been holding in a lot—fear, resentment, anger—in an understandable effort not to rock the marital boat during a mission-critical time for our future together. But to move forward in honesty, this carryover detritus from both active addiction and early recovery needed to be aired, accepted and addressed accordingly.

≈

The first amends I made to Patty were simple, straight-forward...and completely inadequate.

"I'm sorry bubs," I stammered, addressing Patty with a term of endearment each of us uses for the other. "I was really screwed up for a really long time. I couldn't stop and I'm so sorry for that. As you can see, I'm in a far better place now, and I won't ever put you in that horrible position again."

I this, I that. I, I, I.

Aye-yai-yai. What a self-centered jackass.

Unfortunately, this is about the way it goes with a lot of spousal amends: a well-intending failure, an understandable error committed because most other amends—successful ones at that—played out in similar fashion and garnered acceptable results.

For those of us recovering through AA or NA, I contend that this disconnect is a side effect of sound advice regularly given in those programs—insightful instruction designed to keep amends from going astray. We are told to limit the discussion to our part in a damaged relationship without bringing up any perceived wrongdoings committed by the other party. If we were 70 percent wrong, leave the 30 percent that (we believe) wasn't our responsibility out of the dialogue. Even if we believe the other party was mostly in the wrong, we are there to make amends rather than demand them.

This reasonable suggestion is intended to prevent a volatile newcomer like myself from turning an amends-seeking session into an opportunity to deflect fault or project blame—even deserved blame—on someone we've harmed. We are instructed to clean our own side of the street without asking the other party to grab a broom and tidy up their own.

When making amends to Patty, however, my noble attempt at taking sole responsibility for a years-long waking nightmare was woefully insufficient. This is not, of course, because I should have been blaming Patty for anything. It is because, in an effort to assure her of her guiltlessness, the standard "I, I, I" approach to amends was too limiting. I was so mindful of staying on my side of the street that I didn't cross the road to get to the other side. And on the other side was my other half in life.

The relationships we share with our spouses are too intricate and important to tepidly avoid turf-treading during amends. No matter how clean I wanted my side of the street to be, this was simply a far dirtier undertaking. I hadn't merely dented Patty's fender, or cost her a high-profile account, or—as was the case with other close relatives—caused her a great deal of concern over my well-being.

No. As detailed in Chapter 3, I had fundamentally changed Patty's makeup as a person. I had poisoned her soul. Patty was a less trusting, more fearful and altogether angrier person than she was prior to my addiction. You don't erase that with "I'm sorry bubs," no matter how profuse or comprehensive the apology.

The reason I couldn't find the right words is simple: the right words don't exist. The amends we make to our spouses must be a living commitment to mutual healing.

Unfortunately, I didn't even begin to realize how futile my amends to Patty had been until the disappearing act that led off Chapter 7. And that was nearly a year after "I'm sorry bubs." Fortunately, it wasn't a decade later because, as is so often the case in marriages where one partner is recovering from addiction, we needed to experience failure before envisioning anything approaching a solution.

That solution, amends customized to adequately suit the most intimate of life's relationships, saved our marriage. Here's how it worked.

≈

Of all the deceitful, degrading and disgusting acts I committed while in active addiction, the sharpest gut-shot guilt struck upon realizing how deep the damage I'd done to Patty truly was. Basically, the personality poisoning traits discussed in Chapter 3 were condensed into a single brain synapse, sending shudders of shame down my spine and into my stomach.

In hindsight, I'm somewhat grateful that I didn't have this reeling revelation sooner. Despite the confusion and hurt caused by remaining unaware of it (ignorance is not always blissful), I'm not sure I could have handled such a damning verdict sooner. Recovery is often compared to stripping an onion—it comes in layers, leaving some realizations visible only after a certain amount of prerequisite peeling.

There's a school of thought that argues I wasn't ready to realize what I'd realized until I realized it. There is sound logic behind this assessment. Many scientific discoveries stand on the shoulders of previous findings. These cascading, if-this-then-that diagnoses can take a while to develop. "Give time time" is an oft-repeated phrase in AA and other recovery settings.

Add to this the elixir that, in my experience, is the greatest catalyst to positive progress: pain.

That threshold, it turned out, was finally exceeded by Patty's mysterious Tour de Manhattan, which left us both trying to pinpoint precisely where, in the 18 months since my last drink, our lives together had gone awry. It was a panicky pain, leaving me with hard evidence that something was very wrong without the slightest idea of what it was, or what I might do to help fix it. The whole thing was far more disruptive than, say, a heated argument would have been, because its impetus was anguish rather than anger. Patty was lost. And it was my job, as both her closest confidant and chief architect of her struggles, to help find her.

I needed that fallout to find out. The incident made me pause, examine, dwell and...WHAP! All of the stains on her soul, right to my stomach.

Now that I knew what it was, I could actually do something about it. I could finally construct an amends worthy of the most complex, comprehensive and communication-contingent relationship in my life.

Above all, that meant getting my hands dirty. It meant looking both ways and crossing over to Patty's side of the street to help her assess the damage. After all, it was my drug-addicted ass who'd trashed the place. That, along with being the person who knew Patty better than anyone in the world, placed me in an unparalleled position to help with the cleanup.

There is no perfect way to tell a spouse, especially one whose life you nearly ruined, that they are a worse person than they once were. It's like walking on eggshells while carrying an anvil, a blend of heft and fragility that makes some amount of breakage inevitable.

"The problem isn't me," I said. "It's you."

Before her scowl could harden, I continued.

"It's you—but it's not your fault. It's *what I did to you*."

Her eyebrows ascended, furrowed. Her contempt faded to confusion.

And so it began, the delicate dance performed when a couple starts to realize that, despite one partner's sole culpability for their marital missteps, it takes two to tango. For our relationship to survive and thrive, we both needed to improve. The entire street required cleaning, regardless of its filth's single-sided genesis.

The result was an amends in which the guilty party, me, realized that he couldn't repair the damage he caused—not all of it, anyway. Not the hurt that transcended mere transgression into a permeating personal defect. I can fix a broken car, but not a broken person.

Marital amends, then, are not designed to wipe away the stains a recovering addict has placed on their spouse's soul, because that isn't possible. The best they can do is commit to steadfast support as the spouse walks their own path of recovery, even if that path involves another meandering, lost-in-thought afternoon in Manhattan.

Let's clarify what we mean by support. Support is not being an unwavering cheerleader, hooting and hollering even while your team gets handed an ass-kicking. Patty's path could not be a primrose one, because those never lead anywhere worthwhile.

No, more than anything, support means candor. It meant that, for the first time in years—since pre-cocaine Chris and Patty—I needed to be confrontational when Patty exhibited behavior stemming from her Chris-caused defects of character. I had to take her inventory, to monitor and report about the fallout from damage I had inflicted…and to the person I had inflicted it upon, no less.

If you think I had absolutely no business telling this poor woman what her problem was—especially since the root of her problem was me—well, you're completely right. But just because it wasn't my business doesn't mean it wasn't my duty.

Tough truth time: Our spouses know us better than anyone else. It took a spouse to inflict this much damage, and would take a spouse to help undo it. I was basically left to give rock climbing lessons to someone I'd recently thrown off a cliff.

And if you think that's challenging, consider what this process required of Patty.

It is my contention that no marriage in recovery from one partner's addiction can become whole again without the innocent spouse first accepting that their addict partner made them worse and then accepting the help of the addict partner in their healing process. This is an incredibly tall order—far taller than anything the addict has or will accomplish in recovery. It is unfairness piled atop unfairness: a double shit sandwich.

Patty didn't swallow it all at once. I'm not sure anyone can.

For Patty and, I believe, all spouses in her position, a crucial first step is the ability and willingness to let their guard down when it comes to their spouse. This is tricky, because the wounded spouses of recovering addicts typically have a hell of a lot to remain guarded about.

As the addict recovers, their spouse experiences hope and fear along seemingly parallel tracks. The more promising life together becomes, the more both partners have to lose through the addict relapsing.

Added to this is the attempted return to normalcy that occurs in the months following the cessation of drinking and drugging. With her life no longer one protracted emergency, Patty finally paid closer attention to matters that, otherwise, would have been key priorities to an ambitious woman in her early 30s. What she saw pissed her off mightily, because my addiction had set her life back exponentially.

For starters, we were fucking broke. Though smart enough to segregate much of her income from my insanity, I had emptied not only my savings and checking accounts but also my 401(k), and racked up tens of thousands of dollars in credit card debt, courtesy of cash advances that were currently earning Chase Bank a healthy 25 percent annual interest rate.

Money troubles cause cascading marital issues. With a large chunk of my salary going to rebuilding savings and paying off credit card debt, our lifestyle was well below what our household income would suggest. In my addiction, Patty had seen her friends experience joys while she suffered. Now, even with her husband in recovery, Patty still found herself in a comparably inferior life situation, with a dearth of disposable income limiting the enjoyment of early marriage's carefree pre-baby days.

And of course, the baby thing was an issue unto itself. We were both 32 when I got sober. Starting a family in such a tenuous position was unthinkable; we both knew it would be a few years before the idea of having a child was even, well, conceivable. So Patty had to watch cousin after cousin and friend after friend become parents. Always the baby showerer, never the baby showeree.

Finally, exacerbating these underachieved milestones—material wealth, lifestyle, family planning—were the character defects Patty had acquired courtesy of yours truly.

Simply put, Patty blamed me for her reduced lot in life. And the reason she did was because it was entirely my fault.

Let's reserve judgment regarding Patty's judgment. After all, this isn't about Patty being in charge of Patty. It isn't about agency or codependency. This is about a person pushed to the precipice of what she could endure by her addicted spouse, and stepping back from the brink of divorce only because he stopped drinking and drugging in the nick of time. Once there, she committed to reclaiming a life together despite what she undoubtedly knew would be setbacks and struggles as the ripple effects of years of addiction riddled our newly recovering lives together.

But that doesn't mean she could accept all of that all at once. Or even in 18 months. Even when force-fed, double shit sandwiches tend to go down slowly. Patty made piecemeal peace with her meal, which required swallowing not only difficult truths but her pride as well.

Previously, I discussed how couples beginning the recovery process need to lean out from each other. The addict needs to learn from fellow recovering sufferers how to get and remain clean and sober, a process in which the spouse has a very limited role. And though the spouse frequently doesn't realize it, this is the same time frame in which they should start their own road to recovery, whether that means therapy, group-centric programs such as Al-Anon or other paths to healing.

I also remarked how recovery isn't for those who need it but for those who *want* it—that I know a lot of dead people who needed recovery. Similarly, I know a lot of divorced couples who needed to recover together.

Here, with amends, spouses must lean back in toward each other. And they must *want* it, because doing so will become an exercise in patience, perseverance and, above all, brutal honesty.

Highlighters out: Amends aren't spoken. They are *lived*—and by both parties, the amender and the amendee. They require dropping our guards knowing full well that healing will mean some gut punches.

They require the addict to let their spouse air their grievances, many of which they have been keeping to themselves for fear of sending their addict partner out the door and into a bar. They required me to let Patty dump things on me even when I didn't feel responsible for them, knowing there was a ton of other stuff for which I undeniably *was* culpable—a sort of amends by substitution. They required me to earn Patty's trust back, discussion by discussion and action by action.

Most of all, they required me to level out my mental marital imbalance, the hampering hesitance that, since far before my sobriety took root, deferred to Patty as the eternally owed—and therefore perpetually superior—partner in our union.

And for Patty, participating in these amends required dismantling a mile-high roadblock one stone at a time, one that she had initially built to protect her inner psyche from the worst of her husband's behaviors. She had to choose to open a passageway to alleviating pain, even if that meant the possibility—in fact, the near-certainty—of allowing more to enter.

Why? Because in terms of our marriage, Patty's road to ruin and redemption were one and the same, and they both involved me.

As we've seen, addiction is a family illness that thrives on chaos. It involves addicts from limitless life circumstances imbibing a limitless variety and quantity of inebriating substances, then roaming the landscape inflicting a limitless scope of damage upon others. The variables are nearly infinite.

That said, the stains I placed on Patty's soul had twists and turns customized to our circumstances and experiences. So customized, in fact, that only the person who knew her most intimately could serve as a suitable sounding board and, from there, a proper partner in their alleviation. For our marriage to regain sustainability, the poisoner needed to play an integral part in formulating the antidote.

This was, of course, easier said than done. It was a process rife with false starts, hurt feelings and over-stepped boundaries. We trial-and-errored our way to a give-and-take that balanced our commitment to a future together with the present reality. And that reality included stubborn resentments that often needed to be whittled down over time rather than swept away in one sitting.

Living amends isn't starting knock-down drag-out wars—though a few of those certainly transpired. Rather, it entails finding ways to constructively criticize our partners in ways that recognize the wreckage of the past with an eye toward a happier, healthier future. For Patty, that meant folding the permanent upper hand in our relationship and going all-in on us.

Like recovery from addiction itself, this tough-love process was far more challenging to inaugurate than it was to gradually incorporate into our lives. But the more Patty opened up to help, the more comfortable I felt giving it, despite the nagging double-guilt of not only being blameworthy for her lingering issues but now, counter-instinctively, calling her out on them.

We did this imperfectly. But we did it. We got there because we decided to prioritize our future over my past. We got there because we saw stains on our souls and decided to get busy scrubbing rather than pointing fingers over spilled spirits.

Only then could we repair both the damage of active addiction and the warped dynamic that carried over into recovery. Only then could we move toward a union in which one partner does not need to feel permanently subservient, and the other can accept the past without harboring ill will in the present.

Amends are a tipping point in the re-balancing act. As the process played out over months and years, the scale of our marriage drew closer and closer to even. And as a byproduct of this practice, we began doing what the healthiest marriages do best: we pushed each other to become better persons, in perpetuity.

CHAPTER 10:
THE BICKER THE BETTER

"Jesus Christ," Patty scoffed, as I predictably doused my dinner. "You and the goddamn hot sauce."

In my defense, I love hot sauce. It's a highly versatile, varied condiment with a myriad of flavor profiles and heat ranges that give it a perpetually experimental bend—an attractive culinary X-factor. Oh yeah, and if you did $100,000 worth of cocaine, you'd need your sinuses cleared out once in a while too. There are few things as effective as a little salsa picante up the nostrils.

Back in our kitchen, Patty really wasn't taking issue with my penchant for pepper spraying my supper. Rather, she was taking issue with me doing it to the food she prepared.

My wife is a really good cook, a Chinese American who nails each of those cuisines. For the former, she has a knack for impromptu, grab-anything Asian dishes: a fast, freewheeling meat + veggie + sauce concoction over rice or noodles formula that makes even hastily prepared dinners on busy workdays a cut above.

For classic American fare, her meatloaf is the best I've ever tasted—a luscious lump of beef, pork and veal that, somehow, is simultaneously fall-apart light and brick heavy. It is also a literal lifesaver. When our rescue dog, Vector, ran away his very first night with us, what lured him back after two hours on the lam was none other than Patty's fortuitously pre-prepared meatloaf, strategically placed on the porch for our untrusting new pooch. Eventually Vector, unnoticed by us in the living room, devoured the meatloaf and either instantly chose to join our family or simply wanted more meatloaf. The debate rages to this day.

But I digress. In getting into a huff over hot sauce, Patty was essentially saying "Do you find my cooking so bad that you need to drown it out with spiciness?"

That implied meaning has implications of its own. Patty was expressing thinly veiled frustration at investing time and effort in dressing up our meal with specific, well-considered seasoning. only to have her dope of a husband smother her hard work in hot sauce. To her, my hot sauce hubris exemplified a low-grade lack of appreciation for the effort she puts into her life and our marriage. And she had a point.

From my perspective, I just really like hot sauce, and her delicious beef, tomatoes and zucchini over rice was made only more mouth- (and nose-) watering with some liquid red heat splashed on top. It really wasn't any more complicated than that.

So there we were, playing out an eye-rollingly stereotypical domestic scene. The wife annoyed with her spouse over something dinner-related that was really a bit more than dinner-related. The aloof, insensitive husband unaware of his infraction until she hits him across the eyes with it. A bad sitcom moment in a formerly bad marriage.

As nuptial issues go, this one is relatively minor, especially considering the gaping wounds we'd already started healing together. When your partner has retrieved you from court after spending a night in jail for a pants-pissing, license-suspending DUI, getting mildly offended over hot sauce isn't exactly a four-alarm fire.

There's a large gap between handcuffs and hot sauce. And it is precisely that gap—that difference in urgency between the emergency and the mundane—that can serve as a useful measure of progress for a marriage during one partner's recovery from alcoholism or drug addiction.

In very early recovery, a lot is left unsaid. As mutual hopefulness stems from one partner's budding sobriety, both partners give the other some leeway concerning the everyday annoyances of married life. These venial sins, we understandably say to ourselves, are insignificant considering the catastrophes thus far endured, and unimportant amid the combined effort to overcome them. Culminating with a commitment to living amends, married couples in early recovery often overlook small blemishes while working to heal the malignant, potentially marriage-threatening cancers caused by one partner's active addiction and corresponding abhorrent behaviors.

And the result is freeing. As it becomes evident that both innocent spouse and culpable addict must heal, and that the addict must play an intricate role in their partner's healing process, large-scale matters are discussed. Long-simmering, soul-scarring damage begins to be dealt with sustainably, together.

And once we feel comfortable discussing big things, we feel comfortable discussing small things. Like an idiot hubby's culinary faux pas.

Sometimes recovery is as straightforward as literally recovering something—reclaiming a freedom long sacrificed at the altar of addiction. This chapter discusses something married couples partially muted by both active addiction and early sobriety need to recapture: the ability to vent lest their relationship reach a boiling point.

A strong sign that the early recovery phase is drawing to a successful close is that the marriage gets its bicker back. Let's explore.

≈

The ongoing amends discussed in Chapter 9 have helped each partner realize that building a future together means not tiptoeing around the wreckage of the past but confronting it head on. Only then, we've learned, can long-festering feelings and ingrained character defects be effectively addressed. We've begun to unearth the deep-rooted, intricately tangled webs of hurt, anger and guilt that addiction infuses into a marriage. And in the narrow yet significant window since the addicted partner's last drink or drug, the union has already shown highly promising signs.

Once two people who love and know each other intimately start practicing the sort of healing honesty demanded by recovery-centric amends, the positivity is about as deliriously difficult to put into words as the jolting hopefulness of fledgling recovery from addiction itself.

In my first few days of sobriety, desperate and despondent, I finally started identifying with fellow alcoholics and drug addicts. "Holy shit," I thought. "This works. This is going to give me a real chance at staying clean and sober." That's akin to having a death sentence conditionally commuted. There was a chance I wasn't doomed—a *deus ex machina* magic.

Now, after the confusing complexities of early sobriety, amends were giving our marriage a similar "A-ha!" moment. If two minds could share one thought bubble, it would have read something like "Holy shit, this works— and we're going to be OK." We were going to make it. We had a clear path to happily ever after, after all. All we needed to do was continue along that path together.

It's really this simple: since it worked, we kept working. Progress breeds progress in a compelling, ingratiating snowball effect that helps keep marital recovery rolling in a healthy, action-affirmation-repeat rhythm. This momentum is, noticeably, the very antithesis of active addiction's own sick cycle.

If you've reached this hopeful point in your marriage's recovery, time—and amends—have provided a safe harbor to address the last vestiges of unsustainable harms in your union. There is a refreshing, invigorating feel as both members can see and sense a happy future together.

However, a few more rocky channels remain before smoother sailing can truly commence. But with amends initiated, incorporated and consistently practiced in the marriage, each partner now has an invaluable tool toward further progress: faith in the ability to be completely honest with the other in the name of mutual healing.

Both of you will test your newfound trust and candor on the other. Some tests will be passed with flying colors, others will lead to spats. Still others will uncover deeper detriments that must also be dealt with together. The marriage is maturing, along with the attendant growing pains.

Each partner is practicing newly acquired tools of recovery, often imperfectly. At this point, though, the resulting scrapes are mere flesh wounds compared to the gaping gashes inflicted in active addiction. Fights are less fierce and pass faster, as each partner realizes that the other is sincerely trying. Both are grateful that the marriage's current shortcomings are far less severe than they once were.

For Patty and me, the anecdotes from this stage read like a laundry list of backburnered grievances, ones brought to a simmer now that the marriage was out of immediate danger. "Do you realize how much [insert mannerism] annoys me?" "Why do you always have to [insert recurring aggravation]?" And, of course, "I wish you'd stop [insert most things I do here]."

This is a period of minor, hopefully healthy mutual bloodletting, as marital observations relegated to the back of each partner's mind emerge to the tips of their tongues. Each partner is unencumbered, less afraid and therefore less hesitant to confront the other for matters of secondary and tertiary concern.

≈

Contrasting the approach that Patty and I have are six of the most frequently uttered words in Alcoholics Anonymous meetings: "So I keep my mouth shut."

They are well-intentioned whimpers, stemming from AA's introspective approach to recovery. We can only control our own actions rather than those of others, and alcoholics and addicts don't do well with anger—even when it's justified. And far more often than not, the genesis of our anger and frustration was ourselves. We're a subset of people whose entire way of life wasn't working, who were doing the same ridiculous things and imbibing the same copious amounts of substances while somehow expecting life to improve.

So in sobriety, we are encouraged to wear life like a loose garment, taking a more reserved path than our previous ram-your-head-against-a-wall approach.

Other group-centric programs have similar outlooks regarding restraint of pen and tongue. Especially early in sobriety, addicts and alcoholics are warned to focus on the draining, all-important task of recovery rather than waste energy waging relatively insignificant battles. With pasts full of poor reactions, we are well advised to rock as few boats as possible as we go about the laborious, life-saving effort of parlaying fledgling sobriety into longer-term recovery.

And for the most part, this approach works. We stop high-beaming and flipping off bad drivers on the road. We stop grandstanding, backbiting and finger-pointing at the office. We stop trying to one-up our friends and start treating them with the honest warmth with which they've treated us for years, often unreciprocated. And during the holidays, we even try to stop pointless political debate with ill-informed relatives.

Generally speaking, for recovering alcoholics and addicts, life gets better as we get less combative. Most of us were way too willing to jump down others' throats for minor infractions, and, given our volatile state of mind and body, they were often misperceived ones at that.

Unfortunately, alcoholics and addicts don't do moderation well. We tend to take mantras literally, inflexibly. We're typically better with blanket enforcement than selective application.

Once again, we come across a positive impact of recovery becoming a blind spot in marriage. Because constantly letting things be in a marriage merely to avoid butting heads is settling for short-term peace while guaranteeing long-term conflict.

I'd like to report that the vast majority of recovery group participants uttering "so I keep my mouth shut" eventually realize that this doesn't necessarily apply to marriage. That they come to view marriage as an incomparably intimate relationship, one in which honesty needs to supersede subservience for sustainable equality to be achieved.

I'd like to tell you that, sooner or later, they see value in addressing the issues in their marriages that were initiated with their active addiction, rather than duck them indefinitely. And I'd like to say they're more motivated to fix problems in their most important relationship—marriage—than they are with an asshole who cut them off on the highway.

But unfortunately, far too many recovering alcoholics and addicts—men and women with five, 10, 20 years of well-earned sobriety—refrain from arguing with their spouses under the misapplied motto of "I'm the one who's sick, not them."

Many recovering alcoholics and addicts even acknowledge that much of their blameless spouses' peccadillos stem from wounds inflicted during active substance abuse. Oddly, they have made highly effective amends with a broad spectrum of others impacted by their drinking and drugging, but don't see the woefully inadequate amends literally lying in bed next to them. They have, seemingly, accepted permanent second fiddle status as an eternal penance for their addiction, however far removed they are from active substance abuse.

How do I know this? Because I hear about it in AA incessantly. Over the years I've learned to internalize my eyerolls.

There's a fine line between copasetic and pathetic, and I see that line crossed with alarming regularity in the rooms of Alcoholics Anonymous. It's a tragic irony that men and women who've gone to great lengths to turn their lives around can be so exacting in applying recovery's teachings that they fail to realize the most important relationships in their lives, their marriages, are too complicated for simple direction to suffice.

I primarily attend men's meetings, so I hear men ranting about their wives more than vice versa. Still, I've heard women give similar fall-on-the-sword spiels regarding their spouses—a particular brand of self-imposed sexism in a society already tilted toward men.

Still, for the most part I'm hearing it from men. These poor, emasculated souls. Sitting in a room full of other men, groaning about the marital dust-up du jour, expressing intricacies about their marriages in a manner that leaves listeners 99 percent certain such insights have never been discussed directly with their significant others. The sad truth is that I—a stranger, a nonentity save for a shared desire to stay clean and sober—know more about their marriages than their wives do.

And unfortunately, the reason this nonsense persists in group-centric recovery settings is that it is reinforced in group-centric recovery settings. With the exception of "everything happens for a reason" (spoiler alert: no it doesn't, and your infantile spirituality is turning off newcomers), "you can't change her" takes runner-up for the Stupidest Advice Given at AA Meetings award.

In a recovering marriage, "you can't change her" is blanket advice meant to highlight the recipient's powerlessness that instead reveals the advisor's cluelessness. It is among the most damaging and widely accepted pieces of misinformation in group-centric recovery. And it is undoubtedly responsible for many a divorce in marriages trying to navigate one partner's sobriety—especially early sobriety.

Of course, there's *some* truth behind "you can't change her"—you can't really force anyone to do anything. But you can try to help, especially in a situation where much of the damage on their soul was placed there by you. And need I remind you, for the thousandth time, that your spouse represents the most important relationship in your life? Doesn't your partner deserve better than the verbal equivalent of throwing your hands up and walking away?

And walk away they do. Right into another AA meeting, the poorest possible substitute for open, honest engagement with the person closest to us in the world. Why start a marital spat when you can start a meeting off by griping to a group of commiserators about your "crazy" wife again? Why help save her soul when you can sanctimoniously cleanse yours in AA?

Yes, I said sanctimoniously. Because these self-deluding suckers think they're being the "bigger men" by refraining from engaging with their wives. They aren't. They're just refusing to be part of their life partners' path to recovery, and their marriages' path to sustainable happiness.

All this confusion stems from one simple failure: They have not made proper amends to their wives. And because of that, they are not growing together with their wives but rather separately without them. They are literally growing apart from their stagnating, struggling spouses. They don't see that while their tools—group-centric recovery, total abstinence from inebriating substances—were right there for them from Day 1 of sobriety, their wives received no such instruction manuals to heal the wounds inflicted by their active addict husbands.

Why don't they see it? Because their companions in misery don't seem to, either. Cue a series of varyingly eloquent dissertations on the "you can't change her" theme. "She needs her own program" is a typical refrain, one that concludes the wife's solution lies not in her husband but in Al-Anon or other recovery setting.

Newsflash: if AA isn't for everyone (and it isn't), Al-Anon *really* isn't for everyone. Addicts and alcoholics go to meetings, work steps and build networks because their very lives depend on getting and staying clean and sober. Expecting our spouses to showcase the same level of rigid commitment to a parallel program—one so closely aligned with AA that it uses the same 12 Steps—is simply unrealistic.

Besides, as Patty found out during her singular attempt at Al-Alon, an awful lot of folks in that program are dealing with spouses and other loved ones who are still drinking and drugging. They are trying to emotionally detach from someone in active addiction, not reengage with someone whose prospects for significant recovery time are improving by the day.

So while Al-Anon isn't useless, it's a far cry from a cure-all. Even if Patty had found some degree of identification and empathy in Al-Anon, it's doubtful she would have stuck it out because she's not a joiner—a hurdle I had to clear because, again, I *absolutely had to do so*. I was motivated by existential fear. Patty was not.

So what about marriage counseling or therapy? Sure, that probably would have helped. One reason is that an expert's advice is always welcome. But even more so, those approaches each would have involved a key ingredient to Patty's recovery from my addiction: me.

The poisoner needs to help discover the antidote. Marriages are too intimate and complex for nuptial growth to omit one of its participants.

This isn't rocket science. It's not even psychological science—though again, Patty and I likely would have benefitted from marriage counseling. That may have uncovered some hard truths earlier in our recovery together.

The simple point is that you don't heal a marriage by griping about it to a bunch of recovering drunks, or to a roomful of people whose loved ones are in various stages of addiction and recovery. You heal a marriage by open, honest and persistent engagement with the person you took a vow to be open and honest with forever.

After initially messing it up as much as the next newly sober husband typically does, the second amends I promised Patty—the *right* marital amends—amounted to an acknowledgement of the damage I caused her and my responsibility to be an integral part in healing it.

This isn't merely my definition of amends. It's the definition, per dictionary.com:

a·mends (noun)—
>reparation or compensation for a loss,
>damage, or injury of any kind; recompense

The only time my wife's name comes up in meetings is when I'm discussing how unbelievable it is that she's still my wife. That's because repairing something requires addressing it directly, not bitching about it to a roomful of strangers.

And once you both agree to help heal each other through honesty, once you realize that marital spats are just pockets of damage you're trying to clear with open communication, well, fighting actually gets kind of fun.

≈

I've previously shared that Patty and I are nobody's idea of the perfect couple. Some couples come together because they have a lot in common. Patty and I are an "opposites attract" type pairing. We have learned to complement each other's strong suits and to give each other space to explore interests that we don't share (like writing a book). We love traveling and *really* love food. You'd be surprised how far that can get a seemingly mismatched marriage.

Still, there are situations in which our polar-opposite personalities must be parsed to find a work-able path forward. We have to trial-and-error our way through certain scenarios until we find a sweet spot acceptable to both parties—a practice in attrition and recognition.

By far, the most important thing we've learned to do effectively is fight.

Not only did Patty and I have to learn to argue—to be confrontational in the name of marital progress—we had to learn *how* to argue. We needed to become combat compatible, literally for argument's sake.

If Patty and I can do it—and we did—then anyone can. Because Patty and I have two very different styles of engaging in a marital melee.

Simply put, I'm a hothead. I'm quick to anger and have a sharp tongue capable of emptying both barrels emphatically and effectively. I have a profane eloquence that generally makes good points poorly. I come to a fight with knives out and with the jugular in my sights. The words "arrogant asshole" would be a reasonable ballpark assessment.

On the plus side—and this has fortunately become more true as I accrue more clean time—my fury has a short half-life. I've been burned too many times by my anger to let it last too long, a recognition that usually helps snuff my short fuse before I completely blow up. Still, back in early sobriety (even the tail end of early sobriety) my anger-curbing tools were far less honed, and I risked turning constructive bickering into counter-productive blowouts.

On the opposite end of the argument arc, Patty fights with endurance rather than an early flurry of force. She considers her words carefully, weathering the initial storm, often letting me dig my own grave in the process. She counters my barrage of rapid-fire jabs by landing one or two truly hurtful haymakers right between the eyes.

And then she stays pissed. For a looooong time.

As we began to get our bicker back, then, we encountered an unforeseen hiccup: just because we had agreed to be honest and engaging with our marital issues didn't mean we were any good at airing them. Just because we agreed that short-term spats were worth it for long-term recovery didn't mean we instantly knew the rules of engagement. We had to work at developing them.

But develop them we did—because our marriage was worth fighting for.

In a union that has endured one partner's addiction and recovery, the very act of fighting is equalizing. The former addict is "reaching up," declaring that they cannot and will not remain permanently subservient for the misdeeds of the past. The innocent spouse, meanwhile, is "stooping down," granting their once-diminished partner the respect due a competitor. For too long, Patty's hurt and my shame kept us from truly facing each other as honestly as a sustainable marriage demands. Now we were, once again, in each other's weight class.

Not surprisingly, the early rounds were fierce. Not only were we adapting to each other's fighting styles, we also were finally saying things each of us had wanted to say for quite some time, but refrained from doing so out of fear of regression or even relapse. Tongues left bitten for too long tend to be sharp once unconstrained.

I, apparently, was incredibly dismissive of her family—a notion that struck me as odd since they seldom say anything worth hearing. (Based on Patty's reaction, I can report that this was not the best retort.) Patty, on the other hand, should stop mistaking my bathrobe for a cape because I am not a goddamned mind reader. (Based on Patty's blank stare, I can only assume her comeback was sent telepathically.)

On the surface, these blow-ups just seem like fights. But subcutaneously, they were helping to clear away some of the detritus that had built up over years of addiction and into early recovery. They were openings through which some of the long-suppressed secondary and tertiary issues could emerge and, from there, be identified and addressed.

Some spats had fairly obvious hidden meanings. For example, Patty's proclivity to not share pertinent details was a thinly masked way of saying "I get tired of overextending myself for you, figure it out yourself [you fucking drug addict]." These often become recurring arguments, because that particular brand of being fed up takes a while to diminish and, ideally, disappear.

Once, I hit a diner after an AA meeting with some sober friends and forgot to text Patty with an update. I wasn't too much later getting home than usual—maybe an hour and change. Still, it was enough to give Patty not-so-fond memories of me disappearing for days at a time with no warning and no return in sight.

Granted, that probably would have caused a fight at any point in early recovery. But luckily, since we had arrived at a place where fighting felt safer, the argument was more honest and in-depth than it would have been even a few months earlier. The less we had to hold back, the more we understood each other and the healthier the end result. This particular spirited debate ended in tears, hugs, apologies and promises.

Even the seemingly less significant spats are healthy, as they represent a renormalization of affairs. Married couples get on each other's nerves and need to be able to express that sometimes. Afraid to tip the delicate balance of early recovery, we had refrained from doing that for a while. Now, some of that shit just needed to come out.

Healing wounds via battle is both ironic and counterintuitive, but it works. Over time, I grew less fearful of Patty while she grew more accommodating of me. She was exorcizing Chris-caused demons, while I was fighting through an intimidating inadequacy toward something resembling even footing with my life partner.

We fought for our marriage, and we won. And as a bonus, we set ourselves up for even better things to come.

Part III:
Long-Term Recovery

CHAPTER 11:
WELLER THAN WELL

Two hours later, Patty was still sitting there.

This was not a big deal. In fact, it was the exact opposite of a big deal. Hence my inquiry.

"What in God's name are you *doing* over there?"

What she was doing was writing thank you notes for the friends and family who'd attended the third birthday party of our son, Nicholas. And actually, she wasn't even doing that. I knew this because I had already written the thank you notes the day before, a process that had taken all of half an hour.

No, Patty was writing the addresses on the envelopes in which said thank you notes would be inserted. The oh-so-daunting list had about 30 names on it, tops. Even considering the newfangled nine-digit zip codes, two hours seemed a little slow. Hell, the party itself was barely that long.

So not only was my question well-founded (and considering its snarky source, certainly predictable), I actually showed some restraint by not throwing a "fucking" in there somewhere. You're welcome.

Patty is one of the slowest-moving creatures on Earth. It takes her all morning to make instant oatmeal. It takes her half an hour to take a five-minute break. And getting...her...out...of the...house...is...just...*excruciating*.

And no, it isn't just me. This has been substantiated by several mutual friends. She admits it herself.

It's also situationally selective. The frustrating phenomenon is even more baffling considering how exceptionally Patty performs at her job, an executive position that demands her to juggle multiple deadlines and adapt on the fly to fast-changing factors.

It's when she's off the clock that the clock is off. She becomes, in fact, debilitatingly deliberate. Like me, Patty works a 50-hour week (sometimes longer), has a wonderful yet time-sucking child, and often has several side projects going—gardening, home improvements, etc. We are busy to the point of time impoverishment.

But unlike me, Patty exacerbates her limited time through inefficiency. And then she complains that she doesn't have time to get anything done.

Her slowness tangibly affects her. It causes her stress and limits her already-insufficient downtime. It also adds to her established habit of procrastination, because you're less likely to feel like doing something if you know it will take closer to two hours than two minutes.

Fortunately, I have no such impediment. Rather— and as you've probably realized by now—my major malfunction is an oh-so-subtle penchant for being a total jerk. The kind of guy who gets pissed when a beautiful beach on a beautiful day has the audacity to be a bit crowded. The kind of guy who outs his gorgeous, talented and apparently very forgiving wife as a sloth in a book about repairing marriage.

Do I hear about it from Patty? You bet I do. And you know what? It's not just all good. It's fantastic.

Because Patty and I aren't just pissing each other off for the sake of feeling superior or putting the other down. Or gaining some sort of upper hand in a marriage that, though once a prime example of unsustainable imbalance, has drawn mostly even.

OK, maybe there's a hint of frustration and nastiness in our barbs on occasion. But people in close relationships get on each other's nerves sometimes. That's nickel-and-dime stuff.

No, our squabbling isn't meant to belittle. It's meant to challenge the other to improve an obvious shortcoming.

The stage at which Patty and I find ourselves is both gratifying and ripe with potential. I can claim longstanding recovery from drugs and alcohol, and our marriage can claim an equal footing that neither of us thought possible during my active addiction.

We are proud of each other. And if you're at the point where we are, you should be proud of each other too. You've reached terra firma—a sustainable marriage of equal partners. You've put in the effort and reaped the rewards of a consistent commitment to progress. My sincere congratulations.

But now ask yourselves this: Why stop now?

≈

Like no other illnesses, defeating alcoholism and addiction gives those in recovery the opportunity to become weller than well. This is because overcoming the physical aspects of these conditions relies upon a personality change sufficient to eradicate our obsession with drugs and alcohol.

AA members like me might call achieving this mental off switch a "spiritual awakening." Regardless of the branding, extinguishing our infatuation invariably depends upon some measure of self-improvement. Alcoholics and drug addicts need to become better people, or else.

The drugs and booze are physical symptoms of an intangible illness, a soul sickness that makes self-medicating irresistibly appealing. Then, one day we realize our daily doses are no longer a choice but a necessity. We have crossed an invisible line that, moving forward, guarantees that once we drink, we drink too much, and ditto for drugs. The same substances that once helped us cope with our inner demons now became demons themselves.

And then, finally, we are able to quit, to accrue some significant separation from bottles and baggies. For many, myself included, this initial estrangement is the result of being scared out of our wits at the direction our lives were headed. Fear pries us away long enough to dry out or clean up.

But as discussed, fear doesn't last. And once it fades, we're left to deal with the same mental maladies and character defects that led us to drink and drug to oblivion in the first place. Knowing we can never again drink or drug safely—that addiction is progressive, incurable and often fatal—the only path forward is to diminish our fears and faults enough that we don't feel relentlessly compelled to anesthetize ourselves.

We do this with a lot of help from those who have trekked the same arduous road before us. Regardless of the group-centric program, our efforts involve rooting out and tamping down those issues that, for so long, fueled our alcoholism and addiction. It involves being unflinchingly honest with ourselves *about* ourselves, and taking measures to right some wrongs committed during active drinking and drugging.

And somehow, it works. We break down addiction's physical grasp by building up our mental well-being. Considering how hopeless many of us had been—how resigned to our inability to stop drinking and drugging—this is nothing short of incredible.

In the process, we realize this is, well, a process. Our fears, hang-ups and straight-up flaws aren't miraculously lifted upon recognizing and admitting to them. Our stains were too caked on to be wiped away in one cleaning.

Rather, what happens is more math than magic. We find that if we continue to be open to working on our shortcomings, we gain the ability to gradually diminish them over time.

The burning, even dangerous anger with which I seethed in early sobriety is one example. The same thing that pissed me off at a Level 10 for four hours the first time might, if I'm committing myself to progress, register at a 9.5 for three and a half hours the next time. And after more than a decade of recovery, similar scenarios may clock in at a mere 5, or a 4, or perhaps even something resembling the reaction of a normal, sane individual.

Alcoholics and addicts, then, generally have two options once the initial shellshock wears off and the bottles and baggies beckon once again: to become better people, or relapse.

Though no such do-or-die stakes exist for spouses of recovering alcoholics and addicts, per the preceding chapters it's safe to say that some sort of "Recovery Lite" is typically necessary for them. As we've seen, my addiction made Patty a worse person—an unfair fact is still a fact—and she, like me, also needed to get better for the marriage to endure.

Couples arrive at this point in our story—sustainable long-term recovery—by accomplishing two individual feats:

1. The addict got better because they absolutely had to.
2. The spouse got better because they were willing to.

The second fact, I would argue, is vastly more remarkable than the first. Patty had been tasked with healing wounds inflicted by her lying addict of a husband all while ceding marital ground to her lying addict of a husband.

By comparison, I'd basically mimicked a bunch of guys who'd gotten clean before me, and gradually reclaimed marital leverage because our union's survival depended upon it. Point: Patty.

Regardless of whose accomplishment is more impressive (but it's the spouse's, let's not kid ourselves), the marriage once again finds itself at risk of stagnancy.

In Chapter 6, we discussed the faux honeymoon period that can develop between couples in one partner's newfound sobriety. We explored how this sudden sappiness is more a fearful clinginess than anything built on reality. We then explored how both parties must heal and progress as individuals—though with an eye toward the union's evolution. Hopefully, they will ultimately "remarry" each other as more recovered versions of themselves.

Now, a different lull can emerge. One perhaps less dangerous but similarly deceitful.

Basically, Chris 2.0 and Patty 2.0 had recommitted to each other and were moving forward as a couple. This unspoken vow renewal can manifest in a number of ways. For us, both on the wrong side of 35 and childless, it was making the decision to have a baby. More on that in Chapter 13.

For others, this recommitment may be more vague, more nebulous but nevertheless evident. This second sober honeymoon is terrific because it's built on something real: real accomplishments, real change, real compatibility and sustainability. You could, conceivably, live out the rest of your years happy with this degree of fondness, respect for each other and balance with each other.

And leading up to this point, your marital life has likely filled up quite a bit. Patty and I had painted the house, finished the basement, rescued a dog. We'd reconnected with friends who had fallen away during my addiction. She got a new job. I got a new sponsee. We both got new cars. We were living better lives and, as a direct result, better things were happening.

You, too, may have reached this safe space—a point where, if nothing at all changed in the relationship, the marriage would likely last. And therein lies the problem: the insidious notion that, just because you've restored balance, further progress is essentially unnecessary.

It's a seductive stagnancy because you could both totally get away with it. You could close this book right now and probably live (mostly) happily ever after.

But like the early sobriety faux honeymoon, we again confront the misconception that your current happiness represents some sort of final destination. It's tempting to see these improved circumstances as the finish line of the grueling marathon of first falling into a huge hole then, with Herculean effort, scratching and clawing your way out. You're standing together again—and this time on a higher peak than ever before.

You've heard of the saying "Don't let perfection be the enemy of progress." And it's a good one. It basically instructs us to move forward even when 100 percent of our objectives aren't presently feasible.

However, Patty and I have found that it's also important to not let *progress* be the enemy of progress.

I have an affliction that, amazingly, has allowed me to become far better than I ever was before I fell ill. In my mid-40s, I am mentally, spiritually and even physically superior to any previous iteration of Chris. This is because the same tools I utilized to get clean and sober, and to gradually alleviate my unsustainable, downright dangerous rage issues, can be applied to diminish any number of other character defects.

Patty has a partner who is committed to lifelong progress because he's seen it work in his own life, and in those of countless others salvaged from the wreckage of alcoholism and addiction. And she continues to grow because she's willing enough—and humble enough, and unthreatened enough, and unresentful enough—to take criticism meted out from the person who knows her best constructively. Well, constructively enough anyway, generally after an "oh, shut up" and a few minutes of silent scorn. Sometimes the truth, such as being chided for her slower-than-shitness, stings before it sticks.

This same sort of recovery reticence is true for me— and not just because my anger issues can sometimes pop up in an inappropriate outburst. (Though linear over time, tamping down character defects is an imperfect practice. There's a Whack-a-Mole element to progress, meaning we must sporadically beat back bad habits. Ideally the harder we work at recovery, the less often we must struggle to keep them at bay—or, to complete the analogy, smack them with a mallet.)

No, this hesitancy is more due to the fact that, in longstanding recovery, the incline of progress is less steep. This tapering is organic. If a recovering alcoholic or drug addict has made sufficient progress toward breaking their physical addiction, mental obsession and primary personality problems that were driving their drinking and drugging, what remains are less pressing issues. Often, these holdover faults aren't even recognizable to us until other, larger ones are alleviated to some extent. This is one reason recovery is sometimes compared to peeling away at an onion, one layer at a time.

At this point of relative safety, many recovering addicts and alcoholics are content to claim they've "got it"—that they've learned enough in a group-centric setting to take their recovery solo. They stop attending meetings and practicing whatever program they used to achieve sobriety and longstanding recovery. They drift away and go...well, luckily I don't really know where they go. I hope I never do.

Most of them are probably just fine, I suppose. Or, more specific to personal growth, maybe they're just fine with *being* just fine.

I am not fine with being just fine. And I don't care if I sound arrogant for saying that. I want to be finer than fine. I didn't come this far to be average, OK, so-so, meh.

No, I must keep moving forward. I've seen too much proof, too much payoff from the work I've already put in to set it aside in self-satisfaction. Call me greedy, but

I set a higher bar for myself than that. And call me judgmental, but you should too.

But what does this program-centric, sickness-specific solution have to do with our marriage, especially once it has regained the striven-for sustainability? What right do I, a former junkie who nearly bankrupted my wife both monetarily and spiritually, have to impose my prodding, some would say prideful, progress on my spouse?

It's a reasonable question that deserves deeper discussion. Let's explore.

$$\approx$$

Somewhere between Ralph Kramden's threatened domestic violence in *The Honeymooners* ("To the moon, Alice!") and annoying couples writing sickeningly saccharine public love letters on Facebook ("Happy birthday to the best wife a man could ever blah blah blah gaaaag"), arguing with our spouses has gotten a bad name. Through examples both poor and (supposedly) strong, society instructs us to be supremely supportive of our soulmates and to accept them for exactly who they are.

And of course, we should. We should have our spouses' backs and not reject them for their perceived shortcomings. We all took vows, and we should stand by them unless doing so becomes completely impossible, unbearable or untenable.

But as we began to explore in the previous two chapters, being supportive doesn't mean being passive. And accepting your partner's faults doesn't mean you shouldn't try to help them improve them. In fact I contend that, as a spouse, that's not just your right but your responsibility.

What kind of wife would Patty be if she didn't want her husband to become a better person as the years go by? And vice versa? Accepting someone fully, faults and all, does not mean that we stop trying to make each other the best versions of ourselves. Ever.

What I say carries extra weight for Patty, and vice versa. When Patty points out a fault—as she does (and does, and does)—I give it maximum merit because she spends more time with me than any other person. And I know that she has a vested interest in wanting me to be a more mature, content person.

The alternative is to sit idly by while the person you love most in the world struggles and stumbles due to a flaw you know damn well she can improve upon and, by doing so, become a happier, saner person.

Why watch from the sidelines? Typically because you're afraid of pissing them off. You don't want to "make waves" or "stir things up." That's a "sore spot" with your partner, so best to just leave well enough alone. Besides, "happy wife, happy life," right?

Wrong. And cliché. And a bit cowardly. These are all copouts—ass-kissing cousins of Chapter 10's inglorious "So I keep my mouth shut."

Besides, couples in which one partner is in long-term recovery from alcoholism or drug addiction have a sizable upper hand at this point in the relationship. The fact that your situation used to be worse than bad can, somewhat counterintuitively, now help your marriage become better than good.

We have an ample supply of "nowhere near as awful as it once was" to draw upon—a well that gets replenished each time one of us ruffles the other's feathers and, more often than not, helps them actually improve at something. Two people who love each other doling out constructive (if not instantly welcomed) criticism? How crazy!

It's simple, really. Patty and I don't think twice about calling each other out for our shortcomings because the resulting five minutes of fury is so much less terrible than it used to be. It's like a magnitude 1.0 aftershock after a devastating 9.5 earthquake. It's nothing, dear, go back to sleep.

I mean really, if Patty didn't leave me while I had a $1,000-a-week coke habit while unemployed for over a year, or while I was sitting in a jail cell after sideswiping a taxi and pissing myself in a drunken stupor, or during my equilibrium-wrecking early-sobriety power grab, is she really walking out the door when I tell her to hurry up and finish the damn thank you letters already?

No, she's not. And after my wife stood by me through all of the above, the idea that the last straw will be her telling me to keep my fool mouth shut and get off my arrogant soapbox is just nonsense.

So instead, we stick our necks into each other's business, make a fuss, sustain the inevitable blowback, cool down...and slowly become better people for the trouble.

We've signed up for that. Wouldn't you?

≈

In the Prologue, I stated the intent to explore how Patty and I arrived at a "barrier-free coexistence," with a premium placed on being "as unconstrained, unconcerned and unaffected as possible," with "addiction fading so far into the past that it has all but disappeared from the present."

This can only happen in longstanding recovery, and only after you've essentially remarried better versions of yourselves. It feels different between you two because you two are both different people. Compared to where you once were, different is very, very good.

And not only do you have a troubled past for which to be comparably grateful, you also have the tools that you used to arrive at today.

You now have the opportunity to use your tools of recovery in what is, effectively, a post-recovery setting. You're like a once-broke gambler now playing with house money. The same skills that brought success in tougher times can bring continued gains now, only this time you're still ahead even when you lose a hand or two. So put the money you walked in with in your pocket for safekeeping and keep playing. The worst you can do is break even from this point.

In other words, don't quit while you're ahead. Keep going. That's how your marriage becomes weller than well.

Married couples who've arrived at this point in their relationship have nothing to lose by continuing to play the game that got them here. And that game is progress—which, to be existential for just a moment, is pretty much the game of life. In a marriage, letting your partner stagnate is the opposite of progress. If you're not moving forward, you're moving backward.

You both have slightly different yet completely compatible recovery skills, tools you've been relying on and building upon since the very first days of sobriety. They have been instrumental to your progress together. You've earned them, honed them, tested them in fire.

They are effective and sharp. Why banish them to the basement of your relationship now?

Anyone would agree that a big red flag in a marriage is when communication breaks down. Couples get comfy, the marriage goes on autopilot, and they become less attuned to each other. They fall into routine and out of sync.

Couples in which one partner is in longstanding recovery from alcoholism or drug addiction have a tack-on issue to this sort of marital ennui. Out of immediate danger and lacking any true crises on the horizon, we don't quite know how to engage with our spouses. We were pushing each other out of the necessity of achieving marital balance and sustainability, but with that goal accomplished, that necessity no longer exists.

So we can ramp it down, disengage, stop fighting the good fight. But what, exactly, does disarmament look like? What does this safer, lower-stakes relationship look like?

My answer to that is that you're asking the wrong questions. Here's the right one: "What should we do to keep moving forward as a couple?"

Keep bickering, that's what. Nag each other. Tease each other. Goad each other. Plant your shoes squarely up the other's ass once in a while. That's how you got here: by allowing the person who knows and loves you most in the world to help you become a better person and, in reciprocating these pro-progress actions, be a true partner in a healthy, sustainable marriage.

Imagine that arguing were chocolate. Really good chocolate. Seventy-two percent cocoa, dark, fair-trade chocolate. Yum. If eating chocolate every day had helped you two get to this much-improved place in your relationship, would I need to convince you to keep eating it? Of course not.

But when the suggestion is made to keep critiquing the other, with the goal of continued progress, self-improvement and marital compatibility, somehow that idea seems excessive. Haven't we fought enough? Shouldn't nuptial nitpicking be kept to a minimum or, at least, to circumstances where improvement is desperately needed for the relationship's survival? Aren't we now mature enough to continue growing without harping on each other?

No, no, and probably not.

We've all heard the hackneyed definition of insanity: doing the same thing repeatedly and expecting different results. Similarly, isn't it insane to *stop* doing something you've been doing repeatedly that has shown prodigious results?

So no, don't lay off each other. Keep laying into each other. That's what has kept you growing. So keep growing, together, forever.

But alas, it isn't just a now-happy couple's hesitance that can dissuade them from continuing to practice their recovery tools. An entire chapter could be dedicated to external impediments to the "progress by prodding" that serves couples in recovery so well. So let's do just that.

CHAPTER 12:
THE FIGHT AGAINST PHONINESS

"That's not him," I said, simultaneously sad and disgusted. "That's his PR representative."

I was concerned because I knew that the smiling person on my Facebook feed belied the way my longtime friend was actually feeling. His wife had recently left him, and suddenly at that. He wasn't happy—he was heartbroken.

I was disgusted because he is also an historically stubborn fellow, not prone to phoniness or grandstanding. He's a steadfast, straightforward introvert typically comfortable in his own skin, and who seldom seeks external validation. He exudes a gruff, even intimidating mental toughness that, as his friend, makes me feel privileged for having penetrated his closed-off little world. He's one of those often frustrating yet ultimately refreshing individuals who bends to norms only on his own terms, and generally couldn't care less if you judged him for it.

This Facebook photo was not him. It was an emotionally airbrushed avatar, a posing poseur. His slapped-on smile cut to my core, especially since this was so very out of character for one of the least image-driven folks I knew. It was deflating and discouraging to see him reduced to, well, basically what everyone else is doing online. My friend had gone from stubborn as a mule to bullshit artist in the click of a camera.

We are little more than two decades into the grand online experiment that is social media. It is a transformative technology changing the way that humans interact in myriad ways that could fill the pages of this book and hundreds of others. For our purpose, let's limit the dialogue to commentary on one singular, difficult to dispute statement: Relatively speaking, social media is in its infancy, and we've yet to discover how best to use it.

Hard evidence is everywhere, from social media's FOMO-inducing addictive nature, to studies showing that these supposedly connection-creating platforms make people feel alienated and envious. Especially alarming are misinformation campaigns that have likely influenced national elections. Social media's track record to date is one of emotional letdown, electoral meltdown, and a boatload of clickbait nonsense in between.

Even when weighed against the pleasantries of reconnecting with old classmates, or the convenience of sharing family photos with far-flung relatives and friends, I believe social media platforms have been more of a hindrance to progress than a help.

Among other issues, it is social media's collective fraudulence that does the most day-to-day damage to our psyches. It's a simple, seductive formula: As we scroll, we see our friends and family smiling for the cameras, seemingly living their best lives for the world to witness. They seem so happy, so why aren't we?

From there, the vast majority of people respond in kind, posting cherry-picked cheer via photo, humblebrag or both. Online, we've become lying lemmings selling a sanguine scene while our sanity careens off a cliff.

Offline, we encounter an entirely different yet equally detrimental issue: society-sponsored stagnancy.

We live in an era obsessed with the uber-individualistic notion of living an authentic life. We are told we're "perfect just the way we are," and to "be true to ourselves no matter what." The result is an ego-driven existence that makes excuses for personal shortcomings simply as part of "who I am."

This is the bullshit spoon-fed to us that, if we consume enough of it, can convince us we should never have to feel challenged or chastised. That we should never have to take accountability for our actions and behavior and, ultimately, make changes for the better.

Online we are less than most. Offline we are greater than all. The modern world is giving us all inferiority complexes and malice complexes simultaneously.

It is in this unhealthy, altogether phony environment that Patty and I, having scratched, clawed and fought our way from the tenuousness of early sobriety to the terra firma of longstanding recovery, struggle to continue living in truth. Even with practice, it is often tempting to be blinded by the BS. We fail quite often but, thankfully, these frequent setbacks are temporary.

No narrative of marital recovery in the wake of one spouse's addiction would be sufficient without addressing some of the counterproductive traps laid by technology and modern society. Both pose threats to introspection and, therefore, to personal and joint progress.

In a perfect world, committing several thousand words to this topic wouldn't be necessary, but that's simply the time and place we inhabit. This chapter is dedicated to exposing phoniness toward the goal of eradicating it from your and your partner's lives together.

≈

Let's log back on for a moment, because our internet-driven lives create huge hindrances to personal growth. Social media especially represents a regressive landscape where good people behave badly, normalizing phoniness by engaging in it en masse.

Admitting our faults or that we are carrying varying amounts of hurt flies in the face of our smile-for-the-camera social media-documented lives. We are inundated with friends, family and acquaintances sharing only what they want to share, promoting themselves as far more moral, successful and happy than they actually are.

This manicured mass-delusion is contagious. We feel driven to keep up with the cyber-Joneses by building online avatars that are little more than personal highlight reels, a superficial shallowness we would not otherwise exude. Prompted by pixelated peer pressure, we become grandstanders and humblebraggarts, exhibiting behavior completely anathema to honest self-assessment.

Far from being shunned, this ridiculousness is rewarded and reinforced with congratulatory comments and satisfying shares. The full-of-shit feedback loop goes round and round, a cyber circle jerk luring us into an environment oozing with posed positivity that, somehow, makes us feel worse. But for whatever reason, we feel strange when separated from this sterilized, idiotically idyllic world for too long. You might as well face it, you're addicted to likes.

And don't even get me started on the trolls. As an avid freelance writer, I can attest that social media comment threads, as well as those on various websites, are chock full of people who waste time writing diatribes on comment threads. Many of them have been ravenously feeding on confirmation bias served up as news on their social media feeds via algorithm. Among other problems, this siloing of both facts and opinions has drastically exacerbated the already yawning political divide in many Western democracies.

We'll dive a little deeper into societal siloing shortly, but for now let's just recognize that social media has deepened polarization and, in giving every loudmouthed idiot a megaphone, coarsened our discourse. This breeds a different form of phoniness: a fake normalcy in which it's become commonplace to blatantly insult and disrespect one another in ways we would never dream of doing face to face. We must guard against facets of this cyber-cowboyism crossing over to our "IRL" interactions. And confusingly, married couples must not let the oversensitivity they witness online trickle down into a dynamic where they become gun-shy about critiquing each other.

The point is that many of our modern ways of interacting are both addictive and toxic. Social media especially is dripping with envy-fueling "look at how great my life is" posturing, acerbic differences of opinion and people who do an even better job revealing themselves as fools online than they do in person.

For couples who have graduated to longstanding recovery from one partner's struggle with addiction, this environment is teeming with opportunities to backslide into bad habits that infect a newly healthy marriage.

Despite being fully cognizant of these poison pills, Patty and I are by no means immune from them. We consistently find ourselves correcting both ourselves and each other when we stray into behaviors that better reflect a stereotypical avatar than a mature, in-the-flesh adult. Here are the biggies.

"You sound like a phony"

Patty and I are both guilty of everyday fraud in our own ways. This is because our own diminished yet influential character defects dictate the way phoniness creeps into our behavior. In general, Patty's bullshit is the easiest to smell, while mine spreads itself out into a broader array of cracks and crevices.

More than anything, Patty's inauthentic actions are a lingering carryover from both her upbringing and her harrowing, often embarrassing experiences during my active addiction. It's a character defect that was planted by her parents and fertilized, manure and all, by her spouse.

Patty's family is both proud and private. Despite attending her family's holiday gatherings for more than two decades, I am ceaselessly amazed at how superficial the conversations are. They're a group of people who clearly feel love and obligation toward one another but who don't seem to really *know* one another.

Recently, a close relative of Patty's fought and beat cancer, enduring rounds of chemotherapy to shrink and eventually eradicate a brain tumor. Throughout the treatment, Patty got little more than an "I'm fine" from a family member she's known and loved her entire life.

This is, of course, an act of stoicism—a loved one sparing a close relative emotional trauma. But by stonewalling and deflecting questions about ourselves, we rob others of a deeper level of intimacy.

So Patty was born and raised into an "I'm fine" family. Love and intimacy are two different things. Her upbringing had plenty of the former and not nearly enough of the latter.

And then her husband became an addict. A low-bottom addict who prompted her to lie to friends and family about his condition until she couldn't anymore, until the obvious facts on the ground and the burning need to confide in others was too great. Her parents still don't know the half of it. Hell, they don't even know I've been to rehab. Patty just made herself scarce for 28 days to avoid any questions.

My addiction, then, made Patty's proclivity for a sort of guarded phoniness worse. Throughout her life she's been prompted to protect her innermost feelings—especially painful ones—for the sake of saving face.

And social media, of course, plays right into this mindset. Here's a smiling picture of my son. Here's me on vacation. Here's us out to a nice dinner. Shiny happy phonies holding hands. Patty doesn't need any help being inauthentic, thank you very much.

Like most addicts, I have a more complicated case of the bullshits. My acting career is far more diverse than Patty's, comprising so many roles in so many situations that where fake Chris ends and real Chris begins was blurred for years. Addicts lose more than their health, their money and their credibility. They lose themselves.

If you've read this far, you're already aware of the lies I told and why I told them: to keep drinking and drugging. In sobriety, this addict-as-actor phenomenon often leaves the newly recovering person with a poor understanding of who they actually are. Free from the substances that were the end all be all of our existence, sober addicts need to learn what makes them tick as people. We aren't full-fledged adults yet, and need to become them by discovering who the hell we are.

Growing up, late or otherwise, is a trial and error endeavor. In early recovery I dabbled in a variety of personas in an attempt to find myself. The result was a consistent, nagging notion that I was, on some level, living a disingenuous life. While Patty had a habit of *acting* phony, I felt like I *was* a phony because I didn't really know who I was yet.

Unfortunately, this self-deception is persistently peddled in group-centric recovery. Newcomers in AA are often told to "fake it 'til they make it," a well-intentioned instruction that basically means "do what the veterans do." This direction, though, is easily misconstrued as poor advice—namely, don't try to find out who you really are, just become one of us.

It's nonsense. Recovery, marital or otherwise, must be rooted in truth. Luckily, I have someone in my life who frequently knows me better than I know myself. No, not my sponsor (though he certainly has moments of intimacy-based insight, proof of how valuable mentorship is in recovery). I mean Patty.

While my rebuke to Patty's fraudulence is typically "that sounds phony"—meaning she sounds like the PR person she plays at work 50 hours a week—Patty calling bullshit on me generally takes the form of "that doesn't sound like you." From her, that often means "I'm not sure what meeting you picked that up in, but it's not the Chris I know."

To avoid any confusion, let's be clear that this is not a compliment. Patty is referring to Chris 2.0—recovered Chris—not my former self, from which any departure would have been an improvement. No, Patty is basically telling me that my persona du jour is inauthentic posturing. To make matters even more complicated, often my BS masquerades as change intended to bring individual or nuptial progress.

"That's a pile of groupthink garbage"

It is tragically ironic that the World Wide Web, designed to access previously unavailable information and sources at the click of a mouse, has actually made the majority of us *less* inclined to independent thought. Social media is a *huge* reason for this phenomenon. This is because sites like Facebook employ algorithms that learn what we like and feed us more of it.

The unprecedented amount of political discord in Western democracies is a prime example of this. If you like a liberal outlet such as the *New York Times*, here's a clip from MSNBC. Prefer Breitbart? Here's something more your speed courtesy of Fox News Channel.

While liberals and conservatives have existed in their own media bubbles for decades, social media is turning these into impenetrable, thick-walled cocoons. It does this by first siloing the information we receive, and then allowing us to interact with like-minded friends. In doing so, sites like Facebook and Twitter turn our comfy little cocoons into cozy echo chambers. These echoes are music to our ears as we revel in our rightness with allies while defriending or blocking those singing a different tune. We hum along to the ditties we like, fingers in ears.

These echo chambers have negative consequences on both sides of the political aisle. The saddest, lengthiest news story of the 21st century to date—the COVID-19 crisis—is a galling, glaring example.

We are more than a million American deaths into the deadliest pandemic in a century, with many more around the globe. Among other poor decisions surrounding the US government's response, the president at the pandemic's inception, Donald Trump, a) insisted that the use of hydroxychloroquine, a drug traditionally used to treat malaria and autoimmune conditions such as lupus, was an effective treatment against COVID-19; b) mused about whether injecting bleach into our bodies would be a reasonable option and c) vowed repeatedly that a raging, highly contagious disease was on the verge of disappearing forever—that we were "rounding the corner."

Unless there's a cemetery around the corner, none of these statements were true. Hydroxychloroquine has not been proved to be an effective treatment against COVID-19. Injecting bleach prevents the coronavirus only because a corpse can't catch it, but per poison control reports,[1] bleach poisonings went up in the period after Trump's comments. And with the pandemic continuing well into the next presidential administration, mutating into several variants along the way, the crisis obviously didn't subside quickly.

This information is, simply, wrong. And the ones likeliest to believe it were—you guessed it—only receiving news from conservative outlets with a dedicated

---

1   Jeffrey Kluger, "Accidental Poisonings Increased after President Trump's Disinfectant Comments," Time, May 12, 2020, https://time.com/5835244/accidental-poisonings-trump/.

interest in portraying a Republican president in the best possible light.

Circling back to phoniness, in this example the phoniness is rooted in sheer mythology. (Hang in there, my conservative friends. I'm getting to the liberals momentarily.) The echo chamber becomes a receptive sounding board and force multiplier of information that is, plainly, factually incorrect. If you've ever wondered why so many people don't believe in the proven science of climate change...well, this is pretty much why.

The left's echo chamber is equally ridiculous. It is rooted in political correctness run amok. The left's social media landscape is one of purity tests and cancel culture—of sinners casting stones. The slightest microaggression lumps those with slightly less rigid perspectives in with virulent racists, bigots, sexists and homophobes.

I know because I am a frothing liberal's favorite target. I am a pro-life Democrat.

For my sincerely held belief that life begins at conception, I've been called a "monster," a "sexist pigfucker" and, my personal favorite, "a threat to all women." I have seen the unbridled rage of a swath of Blue America that claims limitless tolerance but practices anything but. Online, I have been unofficially excommunicated from the Democratic Party more times than I can count.

These people are among the worst kinds of phonies: judgmental fakers who exclude all other perspectives in the name of inclusion. (See, conservatives? Told you I'd even the political playing field.)

Right or left, such phoniness creates a vacuum that sucks us in. It gives us biases based on bullshit and righteousness rooted in wrongheadedness. And married couples—in recovery or otherwise—have a responsibility to each other to diffuse this nonsense when we see it in our spouses.

Why am I harping on phoniness so much, you ask? Simple: phoniness is a lie in action. And lies, whatever their origins, are what our other character defects, big and small, hide behind.

Phoniness provides cover for stagnancy and regression. As two people committed to perpetual progress, Patty and I are particularly on guard against it. Over time, a union of two professional public relations executives has largely become a no-nonsense, no-spin zone. But getting there took work and the willingness to stick our heads in each other's business.

Discarding phoniness from your marriage requires constant vigilance. We must consistently and convincingly call each other out for playing inauthentic roles and buying into nonsense groupthink. Add a bullshit shovel to your marital recovery toolbox and wield it lovingly yet unflinchingly.

≈

Another modern-day mass delusion is the well-intentioned yet supremely misguided idea that we are "perfect just the way we are." A phrase designed to inspire self-esteem—to encourage, for example, a child to embrace their differences from classmates rather than be ashamed of them—has deviated from its reasonable roots onto a grander stage, where it serves as an excuse for stubbornness and stagnancy.

"That's just the way I am" has become the unofficial tagline for self-righteous complacency masked as proud individualism. Worse, this behavior is not only excused but encouraged, with friends handing us the emotional equivalent of participation trophies for sticking to our guns. Often, congratulatory platitudes like "you do you" only reinforce wrongheadedness. This is nothing more than a fool's paradise where character defects are explained away as personalized perfections. This false equivalence accepts all perspectives as valid simply because they are based on differing or diverse opinions and experiences.

Flipping back through the previous chapters reveals how ridiculous this concept is. Had I embraced this ego-driven mindset I would never have recovered from alcoholism and drug addiction, let alone gradually diminished the crippling personality problems that fueled my physical compulsion and mental obsession. And had Patty and I deemed our marriage perfect just the way it was once I finally got clean and sober, we would currently be divorced.

The day we proclaim ourselves perfect is the day progress ceases. And for far too many people that day is, seemingly, every day.

For marriages recovering from one (or both) partner's addiction, dispelling the modern myth of idyllic individualism involves actions both within the marriage and in our relationships with others—friends, family, coworkers, strangers.

Let's start with our relationships outside of the marriage. Actualizing the understanding that you are not perfect and that, in fact, no one is—in other words, choosing to live in reality—bears the most value and satisfaction in our closest relationships. For example, over the years Patty and I have found that the friends who have endured in our lives are the ones we've long since stopped walking down the primrose path of uber-politeness. The inability to tell a comrade "I don't think you're acting appropriately, and here's why," is the definition of a fair-weather friendship.

In recovery, I have been fortunate to experience how truly getting to know someone, warts and all, makes them *more* attractive rather than less. And as we accept people for who they truly are even while encouraging them to seek perpetual progress, we realize they are—simply through continued friendship—doing the same for us. I find that the friends closest to me acknowledge and accept my personal faults rather than pave over them, and that they also aren't shy about calling me on them.

For me, the biggest no-no with close friends is placating them just because it's the easiest path, which is little more than fear of conflict masquerading as acceptance. Life has enough forced phoniness without us adding more of it to the world, especially when conversing with those closest to us.

Family members are an interesting segue to more peripheral players like coworkers and strangers, because they are a handful of wildcards who we are, typically, stuck with. Ideally, Patty and I strive to have the same level of intimate candor with family members—especially immediate family—as we do with close friends. Still, as relatives are fixed commodities rather than chosen ones, we must operate under the assumption that we can't walk away from the relationship. Therefore, we can't beat down doors that don't budge at first or second blow. To that end, there are relatives with whom we are intimate, and others who more resemble acquaintances placed in our lives by genetic circumstance.

With this second set—the acquaintances category— we largely let "them do them" without letting "them do us." Well before the COVID-19 pandemic, we were socially distancing from this set via an emotional detachment that, on our best days, is firm yet nonjudgmental.

Regardless, we realize this approach exposes one overarching, unavoidable judgment on our part. This is the assessment that the grandstanding, self-promotion and stubborn lack of self-awareness prevalent in society—one exacerbated by social media and reinforced with individualism run amok—is simply too ingrained in too many people for us to do too much about it. The best we can do is carve out a tight inner circle of companions who choose intimacy over phoniness.

And this circle, of course, includes each other. Patty and I save the biggest myth-busting for ourselves, and it isn't always pretty. But hey, sometimes progress isn't pretty. Patty and I police each other in an attempt to arrest society's stubborn self-satisfaction before it assaults our marriage.

If Patty sees me half-assing something—for example, playing with my phone when I should be playing with our son—she has carte blanche to bypass surface veins and go straight for the jugular. So rather than "Chris, please put your phone away" I get "Chris, *play* with him. You're better than that."

She's right: I am better than that. But only because the person who knows me most is comfortable telling me I'm living up to society's subpar standards rather than our loftier ones. And if that sounds arrogant, well, tough. We're not OK with being mediocre. We strive to be weller than well.

Besides, I give just as well as I take. Because the most frequent lecture I dole out to Patty is—and yes, I'm going there—"You need to take care of yourself better."

In Patty's case, that generally translates to "When is the last time you exercised?"

As I transitioned into longstanding recovery, I decided that I didn't get clean and sober to die prematurely from a heart attack, diabetes, lung cancer or any number of ailments largely caused by lifestyle choices. I also decided that, if I could do anything about it, my wife wouldn't either.

A quick tangent: if you're in early recovery, eat and smoke to your heart's content if it helps you stay sober. Lifestyle changes require a life, period, and you won't have one if you go back to drinking and drugging yourself to death. Eating poorly and smoking kill gradually, whereas addiction can kill suddenly.

So no need to quit fast food and cigarettes cold turkey along with alcohol and drugs. Just know that they should be addressed once a firm foundation of recovery is established. If you're still treating your body like a dumpster in longstanding sobriety, I suggest you stop doing that.

This is a societal sickness. Evidenced by the approximately 40 percent of Americans who qualify as obese, most people would be well advised to eat more healthily and exercise more. Bombarded with advertisements for outsized portions of burgers and pizza and candy and cookies, we are told it is acceptable to consume thousands of calories with each meal and hundreds in between them. Meanwhile, our screen-driven world draws us to couches rather than gyms, normalizing a level of inactivity that atrophies our bodies.

My goal is not to body shame anyone. But it's merely a fact that most of us—Patty and I included—are too heavy. All of us have been blessed with two overarching gifts: our minds and our bodies. Comprehensive, honest recovery demands we take care of both. Unfortunately, a facet of societal phoniness is the notion that treating our bodies poorly is a personal choice rather than mere vice.

Patty and I are, luckily, healthier than most—but there is certainly room for improvement. She probably eats better (and less) than me; I definitely exercise more than her. We could both stand to drop five pounds (OK, maybe ten). But you get the idea: go there. As great as it is to be your own worst critic, it's even more valuable when progress-centric self-awareness is buttressed by our better halves.

Patty and I are not perfect just the way we are. The best we can do is be better than we were yesterday. And a large part of that is calling out each other's phoniness. Among other benefits, ridding your relationship of bullshit will be invaluable when shit gets real. For Patty and me, that moment arrived promptly in March 2016, when our recovery became a three-covery.

CHAPTER 13:
BABY STEPS

"Are we really doing this?"

It was a $64 thousand question posed as if playing *Who Wants to Be a Millionaire*. Only it wasn't a microphone Patty was clutching. It was her birth control pills, and it was final answer time.

"Yes," I replied, with all the confidence of an unconvinced contestant. I could see Patty's lingering skepticism as well. How much of this hesitancy was common to most would-be parents, and how much was attributable to one partner's $1,000-a week coke habit from the not-too-distant past, I'm not sure either of us could pinpoint. Was four years clean enough for fatherhood?

Regardless, we were in. About a year and a half later, after an early-term miscarriage that first shook and then strengthened our resolve to procreate, Nicholas was born in March 2016. Five pounds, ten ounces, with his mother's nose (thankfully), my hair (again thankfully) and—bafflingly considering my beady beamers and Patty's Chinese ethnicity—large, lively eyes. A perfect little dude for an imperfect little couple.

He was also right on time, and not just because his birthday is one day after Patty's and two days after mine. Rather, Nicholas was just in time because Patty and I, at 37, were running out of it.

Because of this, our path to parenthood in recovery was, I believe, uncommonly linear. I got clean and sober when Patty and I were each 32—by no means old but not exactly young. Like any couple at such a crossroads, we had emotional (and financial) foundations to rebuild together before bringing a baby on board.

It's understandable that Patty's biological clock was in both our minds as we went about putting our lives back together. This included, of course, determining whether putting our lives back together meant *staying* together.

Everything, then, was a bit fast-tracked. I really don't think we were ready—but again, I'm not sure if anyone, addict or normie, is ever entirely ready for parenthood. We had a decision to make: if we really wanted to be mommy and daddy, we'd have to stay on the right side of Mother Nature and Father Time.

There are about as many winding paths to parenthood as there are to recovery, so no comprehensive "if you're in this situation, do this" narrative is possible. This was merely our route, driven directly and in the express lane for lack of a viable alternative. From this experience, what I can say with complete confidence is that if you have the luxury of time, take it. I wish I'd had more clean time under my belt before Nicholas came around. We'll get into why later in this chapter.

If you're young and married and childless in recovery, I suggest staying that way until your path forward is less intimidating than the leap of faith two people pushing 40 had to take. If you have the benefit of a lengthy biological clock, use that time to rebuild the bond that was nearly severed by addiction. As we've seen in the previous chapters, strengthening your dedication to each other takes hard work and patient practice. The only reason Patty and I dove into parenthood so soon is because the pool was running out of water.

And of course, you may have already been a parent when addiction struck, possibly subjecting your children to a terrifying experience before recovery and reconciliation took root. From knowing intimately many recovering addicts and alcoholics in exactly this position, it is clear to me that addiction is a family affliction that requires a family solution.

Encouragingly, I know men and women who endured bottoms deeper and longer than mine with their kids squarely in the line of fire. More often than not, today their bond with their children is as strong as their recovery. Like anything involving addicts, parenthood can be, at its best, an inspiring "before and after" story that leaves all parties more grateful for good times because they've suffered through troubled ones. A chaotic childhood with a happy ending is better than a purely hellish one.

Regardless of the individual circumstances, most post-addiction parenthood scenarios share a common factor: raising kids brings out even more perceptions and judgments between two people that, in an effort to reconcile a broken marriage, had previously been put on the back burner.

This may or may not include perceived faults each partner has already addressed with the other, per the progress-centric confrontations discussed in Chapters

10 to 12. Remember: just because you've committed to making each other better people doesn't mean your individual faults—and mutual perceptions of each other—instantly wash away. It's an imperfect process and, with kids in the picture, the marriage can adopt a crossfire nitpickiness as we try to avoid passing our partner's shortcomings to our offspring.

In this fashion, children have a way of making previously addressed (or even long-accepted) faults we perceive in both ourselves and our spouses suddenly unacceptable. For two people recovering from a nightmarish past along separate yet intertwined paths, these heretofore below-the-surface disconnects have ways of bubbling over in parenthood.

We have a natural desire to make our children as well-adjusted and prepared for the real world as possible. And in the four-plus years leading up to Nicholas's birth, Patty and I had recovered from my addiction in distinctive ways that, as discussed, essentially made our choice to remain together a remarriage. In fact we were still—and are still, to this day—getting to know the 2.0 versions of ourselves continuing to emerge from the wreckage of my addiction.

Naturally, we want Nicholas to embody the most desirable of our traits and values, but the problem now becomes two people with different (and recent) growth experiences agreeing on what those traits and values are. This "survival of the fittest" mindset we have toward our children can give parents in recovery fits.

Marriage doesn't make two people melded at the mind, and the desperate need for change had altered me and Patty in ways the other often couldn't fully recognize. Maybe another five years would have sufficed for this vast experiment in individual progress and marital refamiliarization to have been nearer completion. But at age 37, we didn't have five years.

If that sounds like I'm saying we didn't know each other well enough to make an informed decision about parenthood...well, that's exactly what I'm saying. But again life—and the myriad circumstances and intricacies of recovery—doesn't ascribe to strictly clinical conclusions. Life is imperfect and messy, and we make our choices based on the incomplete and inconclusive evidence at our disposal. And besides, though the complexities of marriage in addiction and recovery may have eased with a few more childless years, by no means would they have fully vanished. This was going to come out in parenthood regardless of exactly when parenthood occurred.

Because for spouses in recovery, while children are a blessing they are also catalysts for conflict. Let's explore why.

≈

"You'll figure it out as you go along," my sponsor said, so calmly that I wanted to wring his coolheaded neck. That was, I replied, easy to say for someone who had more than a decade in recovery before having a kid.

"Then you should have gotten clean at 19," he joked. It was his way of saying that I had to live life on life's terms. Four years may not have been ideal for fatherhood but it would have to do.

And so far, so OK. On the plus side I haven't made any calamitous parenting mistakes (yet). On the minus side, anything short of limb amputation wouldn't really be calamitous at my son's young age. Making sure a boy gets to school on time, brushes his teeth and eats his dinner doesn't exactly take Father of the Year-caliber wisdom.

My most pressing concern going into parenthood—that I didn't have enough recovery to father a child—still lingers over everything. Because, as my story exemplifies, addiction and alcoholism rarely exist in a vacuum. Drunks and junkies don't just magically become boozehounds and drug fiends out of nowhere. Newcomers come into recovery needing not only abstinence from alcohol and drugs, but also answers as to why they became alcoholics and addicts in the first place.

Normally, then, we are decidedly abnormal. We drank and drugged to dull, numb and eventually blot out feelings of inadequacy, alienation, loss, pain. A lot of us, like me, also have concurrent mental disorders such as depression and anxiety. Many addicts—recovered or active—will claim that booze and drugs saved their life before ruining it.

For many, this warped sense of normalcy began from childhood. In my case, very early childhood. (The Introduction includes a lengthier autobiography; here's the abridged version.)

My very first memory involves the event that shaped my youth. A few months after my third birthday, my mother died suddenly. She was seven months pregnant and only 24 years old.

My dad, the son of an alcoholic father and negligent mother, would have struggled in a two-parent household, let alone single fatherhood. Though an inherently good person, his shortcomings reflected his own parents' failures. Nobody ever provided my father with an adequate example of mature adulthood—and you can't teach what you don't know.

So this isn't to cast blame, but merely to state fact. Faulting my father for my upbringing is like faulting a blind man for crashing your car. Today my dad is part of my life, and my son's, and I'm grateful for that.

That said, my childhood was anything but ideal. The double whammy of having only one parent who himself wasn't raised in sanity led to chaos and confusion. Growing up, I felt that my peers had been handed instructions on how to be normal, then purposefully kept this top-secret information to themselves.

Fast forward to present day, after my early-20s health scare (again, see Introduction), suicidal-gesture-level depression and anxiety, low-bottom cocaine addiction and subsequent decade-plus of recovery. Since Nicholas's birth, I've been anxiously awaiting the day when all would be revealed. Somehow—observation, osmosis, dumb luck—I'd wake up one morning and magically know how to be a dad.

It's becoming increasingly evident that expecting this epiphany is wishful thinking. And with Nicholas reaching the age when—as suddenly happened with me that awful August afternoon in 1982—his experiences will become actual memories, my stunted sense of normalcy is growing more and more burdensome.

Taking cues from other dads has been largely remedial. Emulating them is an exercise in what I already know. Their lessons are logistical: change diapers, fasten child seats, read books, play with train sets and puzzles. Helpful stuff, but nothing the standard father-to-be literature wouldn't provide.

Rather, what my fatherhood contemporaries possess is less tangible. There's a matter-of-factness about their parental interactions—an oxymoronic, nurture-instilled naturalness that I'm sorely lacking. There is wisdom there that is inexplicable, and which runs too deep simply to rub off.

The only way I could possibly have closed the gap between me and my frustratingly capable fellow father friends is if I'd had a bit more seasoning before putting the turkey in the oven.

And as anyone who married a "normie" would attest, my wife's actions are, somehow, simultaneously more intimate and less instructive. Few things make me feel more "less than" than watching Patty, who is so normal that it's somehow weird (see the Prologue for Patty's bio), instinctively mother Nicholas while I stand idly aside like a typical sitcom dad doofus.

Though unintentional, the result has been an uneven parenting power dynamic, one whose gap is occupied by my normalcy detriment.

This isn't to say we're not a team. We consult with each other, discuss pros and cons, and come to consensus whenever possible. And again, thus far this teamwork has been entirely adequate. My shortcomings haven't been consequential. What I don't know hasn't hurt him.

However, as Nicholas gets older, my impaired sense of normalcy will inevitably be exposed. As he goes off to school, over to friends' houses and out on dates, the issues he'll take to dear old dad will likely cause me increasing amounts of head scratching. After all, I can't exactly tell him to do what I'd do.

How will I advise him to handle a bully? By cowering away and regretting it for the rest of his life, like I did? How does someone who had no friends in grade school assess whether his son's friendships are healthy, or communicate the dangers of peer pressure? And how does someone who, for lack of a female family member, grew up deathly intimidated and confused by the opposite sex give dating advice?

As Nicholas's life gets more complicated, the advice he'll seek will be more specific and nuanced. Some of it also will be dad-centric, leaving me up a creek without my wife's normalcy to help paddle.

When those instances come, I'll largely be speaking from the opposite of experience. I'll be speaking from inexperience—or, even worse, terrible experiences, some of which have scarred my soul for three decades running. Not exactly the stuff I'd like to pass on to my son.

There is no tidy ending here. Confusing, awkward times lie ahead, moments where I'll be reminded of my own difficult childhood while struggling to shape my son's.

Of course, I'm projecting, as addicts are apt to do. My success as a father will depend largely upon what I do from this point forward. And of course, it depends on my wife and parenting partner.

No parent whose oldest (and only) is still in elementary school can give anything resembling comprehensive advice on parenting, let alone parenting in recovery. Still, themes particular to the purpose of this book—marital balance in the wake of one spouse's addiction and recovery—have already emerged. Some have been resolved, some are ongoing, and others either barely recognized or still flying under our recovery-relevant radar.

Patty and I are swimming in the evolving dynamics of raising a child in a post-addiction relationship. Following are some of those experiences.

≈

"You fucking make it worse."

For once, it was Patty doing the swearing. Our then-three-year-old son was, well, acting like a three-year-old. He just...doesn't...*listen*. On this particular occasion, he was going intentionally limp while I was trying to pick him up to get dressed, as if he'd suddenly become steeped in the ways of nonviolent protest. No justice, no pants.

And if I had dropped him, potentially no consciousness. What he was doing wasn't safe, and after several warnings he'd earned a tongue-lashing and a timeout. As Patty cursed me out in the kitchen, Nicholas wailed away from his room.

Same consequence, different three-year-old behavior. Public meltdowns, impromptu hunger strikes, hitting, bedtime breakdowns. Patty and I know this is all par for the course. There's a book called *Toddlers Are Assholes!* that, in my humble opinion, ranks among the greatest works of literary journalism in the history of the printed word.

So while Patty and I knew Nicholas's difficult demeanor was largely typical of a toddler, we tended to react differently when he misbehaved.

This anecdote exemplifies parenting in recovery. The spouse with the more checkered past tries to instill in his child traits he himself lacked—missing pieces he feels led to the life-threatening horrors of addiction. Unsurpassed on this list of desirable character assets is discipline.

Addiction is an illness that wants its victims dead, and my job as a parent is to protect my son. There isn't much I wouldn't do to prevent Nicholas from having to suffer through what I endured. If that means a tempertantrum timeout and telling my beautiful wife "too fucking bad if it gets worse, he needs to learn how to listen," then so be it.

As parents, recovering addicts and alcoholics feel an urgent responsibility to teach our children character assets whose absence helped lead us to addiction and alcoholism. This holds especially true for those in recovery who, like me, also had troubled childhoods. What ties both together is the inability to function in normal society.

Earlier in this chapter I mentioned that, growing up, I felt as if other children had been handed instructions to life that I had not received. As I sank further into addiction, a similar feeling of warily witnessing others function normally both reopened and deepened these boyhood wounds.

As a character asset, discipline is an ideal microcosm, as it is essentially a macrocosm. I would argue that the primary purpose of parenting is to prepare our offspring for the real world, for a time when we can't protect them and they'll have to make their own judgments. That requires impulse control and rational, consequence-considered reasoning.

Drawing on the only experience I can (my own), I want Nicholas to possess the fear-based discipline that saved my life in early recovery, only minus the fear. I want Nicholas to grow up knowing how to behave in a normal society, a skill I didn't begin learning until my 30s.

And of course, from Patty's far more normalcy-rooted perspective, he was just a three-year-old being a three-year-old. And my incessant need to correct him is counterproductive overkill.

Here's the rub: both of us are sort of right. Welcome to parenting: two honest people with different yet not-incorrect ideas of what the proper response to a defiant child should be.

More complicated yet, welcome to parenting in recovery: two honest people with different yet not-incorrect ideas of what the proper response to a defiant child should be...while one has the presumptuousness (and sometimes hubris) of overcoming addiction, and the other has the assuredness (and sometimes cocksuredness) of knowing her partner doesn't know normal from a hole in his ass.

Patty and I typically find that, in these seemingly incompatible instances, workable solutions can be found by going back to basics. Couples in recovery need to utilize in parenthood the same tools they've developed and honed to re-establish marital balance following one spouse's addiction and recovery. It is a constant push/pull, an ongoing process of recognizing lingering damage from the wreckage of the past and helping each other clean it up.

In this case, what Patty means by "you're fucking making it worse" is "you're too rigid, you brainwashed recovery jerkoff." (I took some creative license with the second half of that statement.)

And what I'm really saying by "too fucking bad if it gets worse, he needs to learn how to listen," is "I never learned discipline as a child, and look where it got me."

Both are correct and well-intentioned. But parenting demands childrearing compromise, even when two parents have starkly different outlooks on how best to prepare a child for adolescence and adulthood.

Often, this gap is owed to the recovering addict's understandable history of treating character defects as potentially mortal enemies. Right or wrong, my urgency in disciplining Nicholas is rooted in my own near-death, character-defect-caused experiences.

My best advice is to play to your strengths—to find a way for your seemingly conflicted parenting priorities to complement rather than counteract one another.

For Patty and me, here's how that plays out on a day-to-day basis.

≈

"Dada, I want strawberries."

One Mississippi, Two Mississippi.

"Dada, I want TV on."

Three Mississippi. Four Mississippi.

"Dada, I want my juice."

Five Mississip—

"Not this show. Other show, dada."

I was getting a taste of what my wife got far more frequently than me: the persistent insistence of a four-year-old. Nicholas could be more demanding than...

"I don't want strawberries. I want yogurt."

...so demanding I can't even finish a metaphor about how demanding he is.

And when four-year-old Nicholas wasn't demanding, he was doting. He wanted to read with dada, play with dada, incessantly interrogate dada. Sometimes dada had to escape to the bathroom just to get five minutes of pea—

"Are you doing poop-poops, dada?"

Then and now, the alone time I spend with Nicholas invariably involves a mélange of three feelings: love for my son, annoyance with my son, and guilt for feeling resentful at my son. It's one of those unique-to-parenthood combo emotions typically pinpointed only in hindsight, because in real-time Nicholas won't even let me finish a thoug—

"Momma's home!!"

Suddenly, I am chopped liver. Patty, the sole member of Nicholas's Preferred Parent Program, has returned to reclaim her undying—and unwanted—monopoly on our son's attention. On this particular day, "Mama I missed you" quickly segued to "Mama let's go color," and then to the toddler TMI that second-choice parents like me know all too well: "Mama, I love you more than dada."

Just like that, Nicholas is over me and my wife is overwhelmed—all before she's even taken her shoes off.

Wounded ego aside, I don't envy Patty for being the apple juice of Nicholas' eye. I may feel differently in a decade, but for now his unceasing adoration is more curse than blessing. It's just too much and, for her, it's unfair.

It's also inevitable. Young kids usually have an A Parent and a B Parent and, despite all noble efforts at gender-neutral childrearing, I think we all know mama usually takes top honors. Nicholas doesn't hate me, he just prefers her—and that manifests into a major mama headache when the three of us are all together.

And of course, we're all together a lot. So on weekends and most evenings, Nicholas defaults to mama with 80/20 regularity (I've heard many moms get it closer to 95/5; may God bless and keep them). Even when dada distracts him with a trip downstairs to play, the clock is ticking on his next for-mama's-hands-only request.

Fortunately, we're becoming well-versed at relieving each other, with the dual purpose of exclusive time with Nicholas for one parent and child-free time for the other. She'll have a day out with friends or family one weekend,

I'll get a "writing day" (like this one!) the next. I hit the gym on Tuesday, she does yoga on Thursday, and so on.

Besides saving our sanity, two additional positives emerge from our (and especially my) scheduled alone time with Nicholas. One is emotional, the other tangible.

First, Nicholas's clinginess during dada time makes me empathize with Patty rather than merely sympathize with her. And since it's really just another word for identification, empathy is a highly effective tool for addicts since, for most of us, it is this "I understand what you're going through" mindset that helped save our lives. Addicts and alcoholics have a soft spot for empathy, because we felt so alienated for so long that it makes us feel something we had desperately sought: belonging.

So in subjecting myself to Nicholas's neediness, I get to experience what Patty goes through rather than just witness it. That goes a long way toward understanding why she's sometimes frustrated, irritable or just plain exhausted.

Getting the relentless "dada this, dada that" treatment has preempted many a marital spat, because I'm learning what she goes through and, ever so imperfectly, learning to keep my mouth shut more often. I'm no fan of the hackneyed "happy wife, happy life" cliché, but sometimes mama's earned the right to vent without dada getting steamed.

The second, more practical benefit is that, as the B Parent, I'm in a better position to push back against Nicholas's neediness and intransigence, and to start teaching young-child-appropriate discipline. Here, the facts on the ground present an opportunity to assert my addiction-and-recovery-fueled need to give Nicholas some much-needed "no" in his life.

As a result, Patty and I are finding that many of Nicholas's nascent behavioral lessons are best taught sans mama. Precisely because he prefers her, it's less threatening for Nicholas to be corrected, challenged or otherwise unindulged by me in an attempt to diminish his defiance and lessen his near-total parental dependence. And precisely because I feel strongly about the need to instill Nicholas with the discipline I so desperately lacked—both in childhood and pre-recovery adulthood—I am more than happy to play the bad guy, if that's what it takes.

Such experiments in controlled frustration are far harder for my wife to devise. For starters, as we've discussed, Patty's freakishly normal upbringing has yielded a less alarmed, more "just let it be" approach to motherhood.

The other reason Patty is less driven to discipline our son is strictly logistical: when mama turns her back, Nicholas just climbs up her ass. I'm more suitable for diffusing the inevitable blowback—to temper his temper tantrums—simply because our time locked at the hip is finite. Once mama's home, dada's off the hook, so if my failure becomes his ferocious fit, at least it's a survivable event.

As a result, my time with Nicholas is part cruel, part cool, and totally gratifying. As he slowly becomes better at dealing with disappointment—unfulfilled demands ranging from "No, you can't have that right now" to "You can do that yourself, you know how"—I have the privilege of witnessing my baby become a big boy.

Encouragingly, there have been simple yet steady successes. Little things like Nicholas fixing the train track when the pieces disconnect, saying "please," "thank you" and especially "I'm sorry" more consistently, and accepting that M&Ms come after dinner rather than before are baby steps toward his blossoming boyhood.

Every time Nicholas doesn't get his way and doesn't devolve into a crying fit, Patty and I see the promising beginnings to our most vital parental work: preparing our son for the real world. That his maturation also benefits our sanity is secondary, but nonetheless sweet.

It is not, of course, always this straightforward. Our divide-and-conquer technique is just one of many parental plans Patty and I will need to execute as Nicholas gets older. These compromises must now benefit three parties rather than two. Our marital re-balancing act is now a three-balancing act.

Recovery or no recovery, childrearing, for all its joys, can be a grueling marathon. Parenting can be like *The Hunger Games*, but with sleep replacing food (#SlumberGames). But our pre-parent lives in recovery prepared Patty and I for the need to be brutally honest with each other. And to not hold onto grudges when your spouse dispenses such not-so-nice nuggets of wisdom, often with exclamation points and expletives.

Thus far, this has allowed us to stand firm on deeply-held convictions without usurping each other's equal authority over (and responsibility for) Nicholas. For Patty, that has meant tempering though not eliminating my elevated need to discipline Nicholas early and often.

For me, among other foibles, that has meant indulging but sometimes curtailing Patty's urge to provide Nicholas with ceaseless social activities and family engagements. As thrilled as I am to see Nicholas interacting with peers and showered with love by his extended family, sometimes I have to say "enough is enough" to our crammed calendar.

And sometimes, of course, a parent in recovery needs to work on his recovery. If that means I'm at a sober retreat (which I love) while Patty takes Nicholas to Disney World (which I hate) with her parents and sister, well, say hi to Mickey for me while I meditate.

We fit our histories, wreckage and recovery, both shared and separate, into our combined effort to raise someone of unsurpassed importance to each of us.

Know that parenting in recovery means recognizing the intricacies of recovery—the different life paths you've taken in terms of harms and healing that, as firmly together as you are, will always leave points of disconnect. Parenthood will make each of you notice additional imperfections that you hadn't noticed before, both in yourselves and each other, and bring to light more long-ignored annoyances that fester in any marriage.

Children also add emotional messiness (in addition to just plain toys-everywhere messiness). The reasonably linear progress of recovery often takes a backseat to the chaos of parenting. Recovery and childrearing can seem like a poor fit at times because sanity and insanity are polar opposites.

This is all good and all normal. In the last two chapters we discussed why it's better to have it out than leave it in. Once children are involved, our parental instincts to produce the best offspring possible push us even further toward progress. For example's sake, raising a kid means raising the bar on the lifelong journey to diminish our character defects.

CHAPTER 14:
THE RECOVERED HOME

One night, the winter following Nicholas's birth, a friend of ours made an error in judgment for which I'll be forever grateful.

Our friend lives in Westchester, NY, a suburb of New York City. She had parents with health concerns who lived in central New Jersey and who she frequently visited on weekends. She was making her way up the Garden State Parkway when a worse-than-expected snowstorm began to make the roads dangerous.

My phone rang, and my friend said all she had to say in five words: "What exit are you guys?"

She was asking something friends ask of each other: she needed a place to at least wait the storm out, and possibly spend the night.

"One fifty-three," I said. "Take your time and focus on the road. We'll figure it out when you get here. We have food if you're hungry too."

To many non-addicts, this scenario probably seems like the most mundane, yawn-inspiring chapter-opening anecdote they've ever read. But to recovery addicts and their spouses, this is nothing short of incredible.

Little more than four years prior, no one would have considered our home a refuge. Certainly not our storm-threatened friend, one of many we'd largely lost contact with as I sank deeper into addiction and Patty into inundated desperation.

Our friend's wonderful presumptiveness was what really stuck in my brain. "What exit are you guys?" is something you say to a friend with whom no protracted explanation is necessary. In five no-nonsense words, she was saying "I misjudged how bad this storm was, am worried that getting all the way back home would be dangerous, and need a logistical solution, pronto."

Four years earlier, she wouldn't even have thought of us. Now she didn't have to think twice about asking for our help. Nor did she need to apologize profusely, or feign an overabundance of syrupy gratitude for a good deed she gladly would have performed herself were the roles reversed.

"What exit are you guys?" is an assumed license to impose despite the fact that we had a six-month-old. And that's *exactly* what Patty and I want our home to be in recovery.

That snowy night put into practice an ideal Patty and I had, perhaps unknowingly, been working toward as we furthered our mutual long-term recovery together. Our home was a safe haven for friends, no questions asked and no explanation necessary. This newfound normalcy was extraordinary to us given our turbulent history.

Per Chapter 11's discussion of becoming "weller than well" in recovery, since then Patty and I have learned that our past struggles have made us particularly well-suited to approaching this ideal.

Part of this is the company we keep. Our protracted pain cleaved fair weather acquaintances from our lives. Active addiction and early recovery had marginalized our friends. In recovery, the ones who returned from this relationship hinterland are those who were true companions rather than those of convenience.

And as friends who forgave their years-long banishment to the periphery reentered our lives, they found a previously tenuous binding agent: brutal honesty. They found two people unafraid to share how horrible life was just a short while ago, and where we were now.

That honesty is attractive and, as discussed in Chapter 12's diatribe against phoniness, refreshing and a bit surprising. By being open about the wreckage in our past, we've invited and emboldened our friends to unabashedly share their own fears, faults and screwups. They suspect we'd be the last ones to judge, and they're right. It has led to a level of candor and intimacy with our friends that, for both me and Patty, is among the greatest gifts of our recovered marriage.

It has made us better people. I've stopped counting the number of times a friend has stopped me in my arrogant, long-winded tracks and told me where my thinking was off. Fair weather friends walk down primrose paths with our faults; true friends block the road and brace for impact.

It's been a long journey—and I'm sure we remain well short of our destination—but Patty and I have not only built a home for ourselves, but created a hub for family and friends. We have fought the modern urge, exacerbated by social media, to act like our own PR representatives rather than real people with real scars, real faults and real hope to offer others who may be struggling. We have done our best to open our doors, our lives and our experiences to those we love, and they have returned the favor by enriching our lives immeasurably.

The progress Patty and I have made in our friendships is a mundane yet miraculous marker of our progress together, and our commitment to perpetual progress. This final chapter, more disjointed compilation than continuous dialogue, discusses a few others. Here are some of the ways in which we've patterned our lifestyles to reflect and further our recovery.

≈

Before Patty and I made the decision to become actual parents, we made the decision to become dog parents.

In September 2013, a few months shy of my two-year mark in sobriety, we brought home Vector, whose odd name is attributed to being loosely looked after by air traffic controllers at Puerto Rico's San Juan Airport. Eventually, he was scooped up by good Samaritans and flown to a foster home in the New York City metropolitan area.

Last chapter we discussed how parenthood has ways of bringing unresolved issues and lesser character defects to the forefront. This is owed mostly to the increased stresses new parents face, and the desire to keep each other's faults from being passed on to our offspring. Parenthood tests a couple's recovery before ultimately enhancing it.

Pet ownership carries no such contentiousness. As Patty and I began to turn the page from early sobriety into longstanding recovery, Vector provided a mutually loved subject of affection to fawn over, dote upon and cuddle with. At once, he became both a reflection and recipient of our commitment to moving forward together in a loving environment. He took the first four-legged steps toward turning a newly recommitted couple into an ironclad forever family.

The following was published in early 2020 on sober lifestyle website *The Fix*. It explores Vector's role in my recovery—one that also greatly extends into Patty's healing and growth.

Rescue Me

The role of rescue dogs in recovery from
alcoholism and addiction.

On October 10, 2011, I sideswiped a taxi while blind drunk, then sped away into the streets of Manhattan. Police tend to frown upon that; I received a night in jail, a hefty fine and a suspended driver's license.

More importantly, I also received the precious gift of desperation. I was finally scared enough to get sober after years of steadily worsening alcoholism. Despite the disease's discouraging statistics, I haven't had a drink since.

I believe addiction is a takes-one-to-help-one disease. It thrives on degradation and hopelessness and, to combat both, recovery relies upon identifying with others who compulsively drank and drugged before finding an unlikely solution. That solution is one another: a bunch of former fall-down drunks who went from doomed to deliverance, and whose experiences in addiction and sobriety are invaluable to fellow sufferers.

My dog, Vector, is a more traditional form of rescue. He is alive by the scarred skin of his mauled-off tail and the saint-like kindness of the Sato Project, an organization that rescues strays from Puerto Rico's infamous Dead Dog Beach.

On an island with some 300,000 starved strays, the gaunt 22-pound mutt endured hellish Caribbean heat for about three years, competing with fellow canines for scraps and shelter from searing sun and thunderstorms. In addition to his tail, he's missing a toe and chunks of ear. A deep wound adorns his snout.

We have both known pain, fear, hopelessness. We have both had the odds stacked severely against us. Given our histories, Vector and I could each easily be dead.

But we're not dead. Nowhere near it. We're here, in my spacious backyard, playing fetch in the grass and sunshine. Just a few years ago, the chances of this coming to pass were so remote they approached impossibility. The combined unlikelihoods that led us to this point make our loving relationship among the greatest miracles of my life.

But this is more than a rescue narrative, more than the understandable attractiveness a now-sober drunk feels toward a fellow redemption story, four-legged or otherwise. The bond between Vector and I extends beyond the straightforward rags-to-riches tale of two lost souls spared from the trash heap of existence.

Vector doesn't just exemplify my past; he plays an active part in my ongoing recovery. Let's explore why rescue dogs can be so inspiring to those recovering from alcoholism or addiction.

A Faith That Works

Whether it's Alcoholics Anonymous or other reputable group-centric recovery program, a key tenet of overcoming addiction can be finding something greater than yourself that helps keep you physically sober and emotionally sound. Some might call this a higher power; AA, my path because it remains the most robust, accessible organization, would call it a God of one's individual understanding.

People who aren't religious, including me, naturally struggle with this. I will never believe in an interventionist deity who, for some arbitrary reason, chose to save me while leaving the drunk on the next barstool to drink himself to death. Recovery requires honesty, and trying to "fake it 'til you make it" with something as fundamental as spirituality is disingenuous and counterproductive. Still, my road would have been smoother had I shared the ironclad faith many of my recovery peers possessed.

Vector helped me overcome my spiritual inferiority complex. He did this with a duality that, I believe, only a rescue dog can embody.

First, there is his very existence. Given the brutal environment and his diminutive size, it seems impossible that Vector survived three years before being rescued. That island is a doggie death trap; that Vector ran this gauntlet losing only a tail and a toe is living proof that life finds a way. Vector showed me that.

Life is so resilient that ascribing to some Essence of the Universe becomes more logic than leap of faith. There are inexplicable microbes under the Antarctic iceshelf. There are blind fish thriving in the lightless ocean depths. And there is Vector, who spent 1,000 days in a war zone and lived to bark about it.

But it was Vector's rapid rise from frightened to frolicking that placed this newfound faith into action.

Understandably given his past, when I first adopted Vector he was a shaking nervous wreck, too shell-shocked to so much as relieve himself outdoors. He spent hours on end curled up and shaking, my wife and I petting him while whispering gentle encouragement.

Two weeks later Vector was a nub-wagging, fetch-playing, full-fledged dog. He had assessed the situation and decided that these new circumstances had real potential. He was safe, fed, sheltered, loved. He was home.

Vector's faith—ironically, his faith in me—taught me to stop intellectually fighting recovery and just recover. Group-centric recovery has gotten millions clean and sober. Trust the process and the good people you've met through it, and move forward one day at a time. Vector's uncomplicated spirit showed me I was overcomplicating spirituality.

Unaffected vs. Disaffected

Alcoholics and addicts are, by both nature and nurture, an emotionally unstable set. Many of us have concurrent psychological conditions such as depression and anxiety. All of us have fears, insecurities and trauma that led us to drink and drug to excess and, from there, fueled that excess into obligatory obsession. Our physical addictions are, at their root, mere symptoms of deeper emotional affliction.

When we first put away the bottles and baggies, alcoholics and addicts are piles of rubbed-raw nerve endings suddenly robbed of our anesthetics of choice. Early sobriety especially is a period of dangerous hypersensitivity. Had I let my feelings get the better of me, I would have felt my way to a bar.

Addiction wants its sufferers discouraged and disaffected. Emotional sobriety comes with patience and practice, and serves to buttress physical sobriety. The less we let life rattle us, the less likely we are to relapse.

Vector is Exhibit A for being unaffected—the emotionally mature yin to disaffected's yang. Blessed with an animal's amnesia, rescue dogs live in the treasured present rather than the troubled past.

Does Vector have some PTSD in the depths of his doggie brain? Absolutely. To this day he doesn't like other dogs, the result of literally fighting for his life against fellow canines. And he hates being left alone, hinting at potential abandonment in his past.

But past that Vector, like all dogs, is a creature of the current. And his current situation, like mine, is very, very good.

I wonder if Vector remembers any of his harrowing history. I'm unsure whether or not I would want him to. I'm not certain which is preferable: a survivor's gratitude for the plenty of today, or the eternal sunshine of a spotless mind.

Regardless, Vector is an unknowing teacher in what for us humans is easier said than done: living in the now. This simple message is invaluable to a set of people for whom living in the past can mean succumbing to it.

"We're here now," his tongue-out doggie smile says, "so whatever remorse or resentment you're harboring, let it go. Give yourself a break, and give me a treat."

We are post-traumatic pals, two beings back from the brink of the abyss, scarred from the past but no longer scared of the future. Each day, Vector and I walk a little further from our separate hells together, leash in hand.

≈

The Saturday after I got sober, I weighed myself. I was 240 pounds. Considering I'm only 6 feet even, that's pretty heavy for a cokehead.

That was 2011, at age 32. By 2019, I finally accomplished something that, at age 40, hadn't occurred once in my 30s: my weight began with a "1-8." I've gained a few pounds since then, but today I maintain a weight between 190 and 195.

As mentioned in Chapter 12, both Patty and I don't have slender body types. I used to, but Father Time took care of that. She never really did, but was never really particularly heavy either. Both of us are probably 5 or 10 pounds overweight, but we have simply refused to let ourselves go.

There are several reasons for this, and they all have to do with recovery.

First and foremost, my personal recovery demands it—not recovery from addiction but its kissing cousin, depression. I have found daily exercise to be an essential tool in mitigating a mental malady from which, like addiction, I will never be fully cured. It is well known that exercise can help ease depression, and for me it's a vital slice of my recovery pie. If I don't stay active, I don't stay sane.

Fortunately, this abject necessity aligns well with a promise I made to myself early in recovery: I didn't beat cocaine and alcohol to die from lung cancer, heart disease or diabetes. In addiction, I treated my body like a dumpster. Sound sobriety dictates I do the exact opposite.

Patty suffers no such lurid past or mental illness, and enjoys no such dopamine surge from exercise. Similar to the dynamic with diminishing our character defects, Patty exercises despite feeling no inherent drive or mission-critical urgency to do so. Her workouts are more mandatory than medicinal, making the effort she puts in more impressive than mine—though she'd be the first to admit that I exercise more than she does.

She balances this out by being a better eater than me. While we both eat our share of fruits and vegetables, I have more of a sweet tooth than Patty, and also a love affair with all-things carbohydrate. On pasta night seconds are a given for me, and I need to beat back the urge to have thirds and fourths.

Patty is a much lighter, more disciplined eater—and not just because I have 13 inches and 70 pounds on her. Recently, she's gotten into a daily fasting mindset where she eats nothing until 1 pm, with the exception of water and black coffee. This is incredible to me.

So albeit in slightly different ways, both Patty and I do our part to keep our bodies in acceptable condition. Neither of us will ever grace the cover of a fitness magazine, but we're generally healthy.

Caring for our bodies is self-respect in action. It is an outward sign of our commitment to progress, an acknowledgement that working to become better people is pointless if the journey is cut short by a premature avoidable death. Every time I sweat it out on a rowing machine against my will, and every time Patty's willpower holds up against the allure of a breakfast bagel, we live up to the elevated standards we've come to expect from ourselves in recovery. I have come to love our disparate yet comparable discipline. It's a sign that we take ourselves seriously, and have therefore earned the right to be taken seriously by others, most of all each other.

Because, of course, we also live a healthy lifestyle *for* each other. After all, we have taken a vow that includes being each other's exclusive sex partner for all eternity.

How can I put this delicately? Patty doesn't want to sleep with a slob, and neither do I. Both of us value the other's nuptial commitment enough to keep that from becoming an unappetizing reality. That's not fat-shaming—it's respecting the person who has pledged to spend the rest of her romantic life with me. I want Patty to have—mentally and physically—the best possible version of me. She's the one who has to look at me naked, for Christ's sake.

We also make an effort for our son. Because like it or not, unhealthy parents are sending a message to their children, and that message is that it's OK to be unhealthy.

Call the PC police on me, but it's not OK to take inadequate care of your body. Being egregiously overweight and doing nothing about it is no different than someone with emphysema continuing to smoke two packs a day. Or a skin cancer survivor hitting the tanning beds for several hours a day. Or any other foolish thing anathema to taking proper care of the invaluable, indispensable and inevitably perishable God-given gift our bodies truly are. We only get one and, sadly, too many of us are going to find that out too late.

It says a lot about where we are as a society that any of what I just wrote is even remotely controversial. It's a shame that oversensitivity has dwarfed proven science and common sense. It's a shame that many are more concerned with protecting their feelings than their health.

But that's where we are, and this framework is not a foundation for recovery—personal, marital or otherwise. Recovered people take care of their bodies, and recovered couples do so, in part, as a means of taking care of their partners and children. Living a healthy lifestyle exemplifies recovery and, for me and Patty, it has become synonymous with it.

≈

"*No comprehende*," I said, showcasing my inability even to say "I don't understand" (*no comprende*) correctly.

Until the COVID-19 pandemic put pretty much everything on pause, Patty and I had been attempting something we've proven hilariously awful at: learning a new language. We chose Spanish since it is by far the most useful secondary language in the United States, and because we have an affinity for Latin American travel.

Sometimes progress is nothing more than doing something you've always wanted to do, albeit terribly. We're simply not linguistically inclined. Still we were trying—or, at least, trying to try.

Or we were until about March 2020.

As contagion and lockdown spread across the country and the world, things sadly and suddenly became anything but normal. Hundreds of thousands of people dead, tens of millions more unemployed. Many things were placed on hold, in-person Spanish tutor included.

For Patty and me, who both service essential industries, COVID-19 actually meant more work. It also meant piecing together childcare, procuring groceries and other household essentials from various online sources and tending to each other's frequent freakouts as the situation steadily deteriorated.

This was not a time for significant progress. This was a time to lean on the progress we'd already made—to withdraw some of our accrued recovery and press through an emergency neither of us (and really, no one at all) had ever experienced.

We were, and will continue to be, OK. And considering what so many other folks went through during the pandemic, OK is exceptional.

I devised a workable home workout regimen, and stayed connected to AA through meetings on Zoom and extra contact with my sponsor and sponsees. Patty tended to the extra needs of relatives—including a grieving aunt who lost her husband to COVID—and threw herself into household projects from landscaping to an exterior paint job to renovated bathrooms. Both of us took care to be mindful of each other's fears and sensitivities during such a difficult time. And individually, we carved out space for the sort of self-love crucial to steeling oneself for an indefinite period of discomfort, disruption and heightened vigilance.

So we took a break from butchering the Spanish language. The servers at our favorite Latin restaurants will have to wait to hear us mutilate their native tongue while ordering some *lechon asado con frijoles negros y maduros*, which I can find more than a dozen wonderful ways to mispronounce.

What's important is that we knew we'd get back there. Back to life. Back to progress. And for that matter, back to Costa Rica and Panama. We have our eyes on Argentina and Colombia, too.

And we'll get elsewhere. We've been to more than a dozen countries together, and have every intention of visiting dozens more. Luckily, we're far better at traveling than Spanish. I have a background in travel publicity, which has made me an exemplary itinerary planner. For her part, Patty is equally talented at shooting my extensively researched plans to hell.

My point is not to brag about our ability to travel, but that we get to do fun stuff together that furthers our progress as individuals and our bond as a couple. We get to look forward to undiscovered roads because we've left the past in the dust and grown. We have reached this place because we've both agreed that it is not a final destination.

We have recovered and we stay that way by continuing to expand our horizons. We appreciate this opportunity because we remember a time when progress meant self-preservation—mere survival—rather than seemingly superfluous self-improvement.

We hope you get there, too. We wish you a happy, healthy ever after—a life together forever in perpetual progress.

EPILOGUE

As I was writing this book, all hell broke loose.

For us, it started with a phone call from paradise. We were vacationing in the Florida Keys in early March 2020 when an emerging crisis reached a critical mass.

"I think we have to cancel it," I told Patty. The "it" was our son's fourth birthday party, and the reason, of course, was the new virus spreading rapidly across the country. There's always next year, we figured.

As the COVID-19 pandemic has shown in devastating detail, we were very right to cancel, and very wrong about the 12-month raincheck. Since then, a disease named for 2019 has stretched into 2022 and beyond.

More than a million Americans are dead. Tens of millions have been thrown out of work. Healthcare systems and essential workers and supply chains and pretty much everyone around the globe is overwhelmed and exhausted.

COVID-19's worldwide wreckage impacted nearly everything—including two issues near and dear to this book: addiction and divorce.

In the United States, COVID-19 dragged drug statistics past a macabre milestone, one the country had been approaching for years: 100,000 drug deaths in a 12-month span. Among other markers, the share of opioid-related deaths climbed from two-thirds to three-fourths—some 75,000 dead—despite widespread proliferation of the miracle overdose-reversal medicine Narcan.

As Zoom rooms replaced in-person meetings of Alcoholics Anonymous, Narcotics Anonymous and other group-centric recovery programs, newcomers had it particularly rough. Those attempting to make an honest go at quitting alcohol and drugs often struggled to forge the "takes one to know one" bonds that form foundations of recovery. There are facets of recovery programs—handshakes and hugs, eye contact and knowing nods, bad coffee and good company—that are exceedingly difficult to replicate online.

The drug-related deaths and stunted recovery reflected a deeper problem: isolated and scared, the world was suffering an unprecedented mental health crisis. And since medical resources were understandably focused on physical needs rather than mental anguish, this suffering went woefully under-addressed.

National Public Radio found that nearly a quarter of Americans were experiencing signs of depression—triple the average number. An Associated Press poll found about half the country showing some signs of depression or anxiety. Precisely how much of this was clinical and how much was simply situation-appropriate mortification, we'll likely never know. COVID-19 was, it seemed, ruining everything before our eyes; the idea that we were supposed to be whistling dixie past the mass graves was silly. Of course we were down.

COVID-19 also ruined relationships. In a nation already hopelessly divided, measures to combat the pandemic such as vaccines and masks became unlikely political symbols. Family and friends feuded over what constituted safety in a dangerous time. As in-person gatherings diminished or disappeared altogether, this discord now played out over social media—which, as we've discussed, tends to bring out the worst in us. We unfriended online and disassociated IRL. Our circles shrank.

Meanwhile, nuclear families got an unrequested taste of nuclear fallout. Sheltered in place together as hospitals filled and the hospitality sector failed, escape required braving a shattered, shuttered apocalyptic landscape. We spent more time at home, in close quarters with those closest to us, than ever before.

For those fortunate enough to make a living from our laptops, at first the extra home and family time was a novelty. But soon, necessity became the mother of irritation. We were restless and discontent—and within direct firing range of our immediate family.

For many families, the flip side of too much isolation was too much congregation. Working and eating and binge watching and exercising at home, we got on each other's nerves. And spouses—already attuned to each other's foibles and idiosyncrasies—typically topped the shit list. Wilting away at home, for many the grass looked a lot greener on the other side of our locked, locked-down doors.

For proof, we need look no further than the spike in divorces—a sign that married couples were not only sick of the protracted pandemic but also sick of one another. It was reported[2] that after just a few months of widespread lockdowns, divorces in the United States saw a 34 percent year-on-year increase, with even newlyweds separating at double the usual rate.

A December 2020 BBC article[3] cited a report from the UK's largest family law firm that found divorce inquiries had climbed an astounding 122 percent since the outbreak of COVID-19, with three-quarters of couples stating things were copasetic prior to the pandemic.

For many, then, marriage during COVID-19 wasn't too much of a good thing. It was too much of a "good enough" thing that, once the dynamics shifted and they were smushed further into each other's personal spaces, was no longer sustainable. COVID-19 likely wasn't a cause of their marital misgivings, but rather a catalyst. It forced them to co-exist in close quarters indefinitely, and to look at each other under an unforgiving microscope. Many saw more than enough to want out.

Patty and I have an altogether different COVID-19 story. While too many others were drawing up divorce papers, we were drawing lines in the sand, together. First and foremost, we mutually determined what defined safe, responsible living for us amid a landscape where the parameters were nebulous and ever-evolving. We agreed upon what we were and were not comfortable with, and

2   Mollie Moric, "US Divorce Rates Soar during COVID-19 Crisis," Legal Templates, July 29, 2020. https://legaltemplates. net/resources/personal-family/divorce-rates-covid-19.

3   Maddy Savage, "Why the Pandemic Is Causing Spikes in Break-ups and Divorces," BBC, December 7, 2020. https:// www.bbc.com/worklife/article/20201203-why-the- pandemic-is-causing-spikes-in-break-ups-and-divorces.

held firm to those positions throughout the worst of the pandemic. By setting these rules of engagement with the outside world, we limited the likelihood of contracting COVID-19 and, if we did catch it, knew that it wasn't through any breach of predefined protocol.

From the beginning, we knew there was progress—if not an end—in sight. As vaccines for adults proved promising in clinical trials, we looked toward spring of 2021 as the first step toward normalcy. From there, we anxiously awaited vaccine availability for our son, Nicholas, who was thankfully now five and therefore eligible. We are grateful that Nicholas remained COVID-free through two months of in-person kindergarten leading up to his early-November 2021 inoculation.

But these are mere logistics. Patty and I didn't avoid a marriage-threatening experience during a protracted emergency because we're good planners. We avoided a marriage-threatening experience during COVID-19 because we were experienced with—and prepared for—such long-term emergencies.

Of course, timing played a big part. When COVID-19 came along, I was eight years clean and sober. I'd had ample time to recover from alcoholism and drug addiction, and our marriage had had ample time to recover from the seismic damage of both active addiction and its ground-shifting aftershocks.

By 2020, we were already weller than well—and getting weller by the day. We had overcome an existential threat to both my life and our marriage. We had done so by committing to a progress-yielding process requiring each of us to help the other clean up the mess I'd created. I swallowed my guilt and moved forward. Patty swallowed her pride and innocence and did the same.

Our recovery tools were battle-tested and mission-ready. So when the crisis of the century struck, we responded to the added stress by banding together rather than falling apart.

Most couples had never been through something as personally horrifying as a protracted pandemic. Having survived and recovered from my addiction, however, Patty and I were well-versed in tragedy and trauma. And this time, the crisis was one neither of us had created.

Did we get on each other's nerves during COVID-19? Absolutely. That's what married couples do. But we came nowhere close to anything resembling a breaking point. We were in this together because we knew our best path forward involved each other.

Having previously adapted to evolving marital landscapes, we soon found our COVID-19 stride. We stayed out of each other's hair during workdays, set aside one-on-one time with Nicholas and, perhaps most importantly, gave each other the necessary gift of personal space. As unfair as it sounds, while others were barely surviving the pandemic, we were thriving in it.

And seemingly like the pandemic, this story doesn't have a conclusion. Its happy ending is the distinct lack of one. But some parting thoughts are in order.

Addicts: Remember that you are not only redeemable, but invaluable. That you can and must remain clean and sober, both for your own survival and for your marriage's. And that once recovery takes root, its tendrils must first touch then envelop your partner in an ongoing process that heals each of you. You made your spouse a worse person in active addiction, and must work to reverse that damage in an equally active recovery. In doing so, you will move beyond mere recovery into something new, refreshing and altogether better, together.

Spouses: Remember that no one experiences such prolonged trauma without having their souls stained indefinitely. Remember that none of your partner's addiction was your fault—but that, for the marriage to recover, you both must heal from these single-sourced wounds. And remember that intricately involving your spouse in this process will pay marriage-saving, lifelong dividends. It may be a lengthy tunnel, but its far-off light shines ever brighter as you become better versions of yourselves, together.

As they say in Alcoholics Anonymous, we have a nice way of closing. May your recovery together be long, slow and ceaseless.